"I have been a rehab nurse  sustained a spinal cord inju sounding board, and more. injury can be very intense and life shattering. Shelly made my job easy, as she was always willing to learn and try alternate ways to be as independent as possible without ever giving up on herself. Shelly is always ready to learn the next step and was and still is proud of every accomplishment she makes no matter how small or large. She does not see barriers, she sees opportunities. She has a great deal of compassion for anyone and everyone and sees the good in them. Reading Shelly's book brought tears to my eyes for many reasons. I don't think I understood the depth of impact I had in her recovery process and life. Shelly was and still is a bright light in my life and in the lives of my family members. For Shelly to allow others insight into her journey, she has allowed us the privilege to fully delve into her challenges and triumphs. Shelly would call me to let me know what she was doing or moving, and I would be ecstatic at her progress! Her tenacity and perseverance is an example for all who face challenges and adversity. I am so happy she has found Tracy and is able to live life to the fullest! I was privileged to be her nurse and now I can say I am honored to consider her my friend.
Love you bunches!"
Nancy Lokey, RN, CRRN, CBIS, and PM&R Nurse Coordinator

"I met Shelly years ago at HGAC, in Johnstown, PA. I met a pretty girl with long blond hair, and my first thought was, how is she going to comb that hair. It didn't take me long to figure out that she is a fighter. She would come to me with an idea, and I would think to myself, lets figure it out. Before I knew it I was saying that out loud because there was no stopping her, the more she'd achieved the more she wanted to do herself. My goal for everyone is complete independence, which worked out well because there is no stopping her. Shelly has faith and will that are so strong that she can't be stopped. She is also someone I'm proud to call my friend."
Jane Schneider COTA/L

"*Standing Tall* is an amazing share of Shelly's journey to self-love and self-compassion! Through it, she shows us that profound gratitude and intentionally growing into who we really are brings healing on ALL levels. What a blessing and gift to give the world, especially for those with paralysis from spinal cord injury!"
-- Kay Lathrop, Author of Amplified Agility, Producer/Host of the Defy Injury Podcast and Co-Founder of Amplified Agility, LLC.

"How does beauty come from ashes? How does peace come from chaos? How do you climb out of a pit? Does faith really play a part in recovery? Read along with Shelly as she courageously tackles each obstacle with positive grit. You will come away encouraged, knowing all things are possible with God. It's an amazing read! Shelly's life combines positive gratitude, faith, and courage in the face of overwhelming odds. It has been a privilege to have a small part in her awesome life. What would have been an ending for some people was only the beginning for Shelly ... and she's still reaching for maximum potential!"
-- *Audrey Shisler, PT*

"What an amazing journey you have been on. And you certainly deserve all the credit for being persistent in seeking out the care and treatment you felt was best for you. I'm so glad to hear that you are continuing to improve. It is good for health care professionals to understand that all patients are different, heal and progress differently, and need different things from us. Your story is a great reminder to never give up on yourself and for us to never give up on our patients!
God Bless you!"
-- *Jennifer Kopp, Physical Therapist, Hanover Hospital*

Shelly's book, *Standing Tall*, is an inspirational story of her faithful journey from helplessness and hopelessness to independence and gratitude It is a true story of physical, emotional, and spiritual transformation. I had the pleasure of working with Shelly at her home following discharge from rehab at Hershey Medical Center. Initially my primary focus was on home modifications and activity adaptations to improve independence with her daily activities; Shelly was determined to regain use of her hands to achieve this independence. She showed determination and perseverance, spending hours on her home exercise program to achieve her personal goals. The progress she has made in her recovery is amazing. On July 18, 2017, she shared that she walked 58 feet....Shelly is not only STANDING TALL, she's MOVING FORWARD!
--*Allison Myers, OTR/L*

Standing Tall
The Healing Power of Gratitude

By Shelly Kerchner

Standing Tall is my story of overcoming adversity through
maintaining an attitude of patience, gratitude, and grit.
This is a story of love, faith, determination, and healing. My hope is
that it will give hope to others with spinal cord injuries, teaching
them to celebrate each small achievement.

Copyright © 2017 Shelly Kerchner

All Rights Reserved.

No part of this book may be reproduced, scanned, or distributed in any printed or electronic form without prior written permission of both the author and the publisher. Please purchase only authorized electronic editions, and do not participate in or encourage electronic piracy of copyrighted materials. Your support of the author's rights is appreciated.

Published by Readerplace, Inc.
www.readerplace.com

Printed by CreateSpace

ISBN 978-1547255894

Cover Photo by Mark Mathew Braunstein

Start by doing what's necessary; then do what's possible; and suddenly you are doing the impossible. -- St Francis of Assisi

Congressional Record

PROCEEDINGS AND DEBATES OF THE 115th CONGRESS, FIRST SESSION

WASHINGTON, FRIDAY, SEPTEMBER 8, 2017

House of Representatives

RECOGNIZING SHELLY KERCHNER FOR RECEIVING A PERSONAL ACHIEVEMENT AWARD FROM THE HEALTHSOUTH REHABILITATION HOSPITAL OF ALTOONA

HON. BILL SHUSTER
OF PENNSYLVANIA
IN THE HOUSE OF REPRESENTATIVES

Mr. Speaker, I rise today to recognize Shelly Kerchner, one of the winners of the 24th annual Personal Achievement Award from the HealthSouth Rehabilitation Hospital of Altoona. This award is given to encourage and recognize those who have made an outstanding effort to deal with or overcome a disability. This year, Shelly has earned that distinction.

Shelly's life changed eleven years ago in 2006 with she fell down a flight of stairs, suffering a devastating spinal cord injury. She was only able to move her eyes and had weak movement in both of her hands. Shelly's medical prognosis was bleak, indicating she would never walk again or use her hands. Yet, through perseverance, hard work and dedication she proved that grim forecast wrong.

Today, Shelly is now walking with braces and a rolling walker and is independent with her everyday tasks. She cooks, cleans, drives, practices yoga and is an author. She is said to be an inspiration to many people through her Internet blog and her published book – Standing Tall: The Healing Power of Gratitude.

I am humbled to recognize the truly impressive recovery Shelly has made. Her strength and positivity in the face of such adversity is remarkable. As such, it is my pleasure to wish Shelly the best as she continues to reclaim her health and life.

Acknowledgements

All of us have individuals who have helped love, guide, and protect us, and I would like to take this time to thank a few.

Thank you to my partner Tracy, for supporting me in my writing endeavor and pursuit of obtaining my goals in my continued recovery. Your love and commitment to me makes my recovery a much easier process. Thank you for never trying to impede my progress and for supporting all my creative and somewhat crazy ideas even when they seemed a bit risky! I would not be where I am today if it wasn't for your love and support!

Next, I would like to express my sincere gratitude to Nancy Derks Lokey, RN, CRRN, CBIS, and PM&R Nurse Coordinator, who was my nurse at Hershey Medical Center. Even if you were unsure of my abilities, thank you for NEVER letting me know that. I remember the day you walked in my room saying "today we are going to learn how to cath (catherize)". I thought it was impossible with only having a tenodesis grip, but your determination and positive approach was contagious, and one by one you helped me make and reach new goals. Half of my battle was lessened because of your "can do" attitude, and I will be forever grateful to you. Thank you, Nancy.

Next would be my physical therapist Audrey Cox Shisler, who worked with me after I was discharged. Your faith and commitment to helping me accomplish my goals enabled me to face my challenges and find a new self-confidence I didn't know I had. I found out Nancy and Audrey worked together for many years at the Elizabethtown Rehabilitation Hospital, in Pennsylvania. I was blessed with the best!

Thank you, Allison Myers, who was my occupational therapist. You spent hours moving my fingers and hands until I could start moving them myself.

Lastly I would like to thank Kay Lathrop, creator and producer of the Defy Injury podcast (defyinjury.com), for encouraging and gently guiding me to fulfill my dreams of writing my book. Your commitment to improving the lives of those of us who have suffered an SCI has been unwavering and steadfast, and I love your Spirit. Thank you for working with us to develop a better treatment and program plan for individuals with SCI.

I was blessed to have been surrounded by a few positive and uplifting women who believed in me and my abilities. Unlike the doctors, they never told me I would never.... Nor was I told "At 18 months you will stop healing." They believed in our body's amazing ability to heal, and more importantly, they believed in me. I'm thankful for their encouragement and for believing in me when I wasn't quite sure of myself. All of us have two choices in life: to help either build up, or to contaminate - thank you for building me up.

Thank you to my editor John who helped me realize my goal of writing my book. I still cannot believe this has come to fruition. Thank you for your commitment, confidence and for sharing this time with me!

Table of Contents

Acknowledgements 3
Table of Contents 5
List of Illustrations 7
Foreword 9
Chapter 1.   My Purpose 13
Chapter 2.   Where I Came From 17
Chapter 3.   Anorexia and Alcohol 25
Chapter 4.   Troubled Love 29
Chapter 5.   The End, and the Beginning 31
Chapter 6.   Manifestation of Power 35
Chapter 7.   Pitiful to Powerful 39
Chapter 8.   Going Home 43
Chapter 9.   Time to Leave 45
Chapter 10. Going It Alone 51
Chapter 11. Moving Again 55
Chapter 12. Finding Tracy 63
Chapter 13. AA Power 67
Chapter 14. Paddling and Standing 69
Chapter 15. I Am Stronger than My Struggles 73
Chapter 16. My New Normal 77
Chapter 17. Alternative Healing 81
Chapter 18. Cultivating Gratitude 83

Chapter 19.   Accept, Adjust, and Move On, or Fight, Resist, and be Discouraged   87

Chapter 20.   The Reason 91
 Finally I See 91
 Before You Start Your Day 92

Chapter 21.   Walking at Last! 93

Chapter 22.   My Next Journey: Braces and a New Chair 97
 Being Mindful 101
 Practicing Mindfulness 103
 Cherishing Each Step: A Chronology 105

Chapter 23.   Tips to Make Life Easier, and Things I Wish I Had Done Sooner to Accelerate My Healing 111

Chapter 24.   Call to Action 113
 Appendix A: My Poems 119
 Appendix B: My Journal 121
 Appendix C: My Walking Record 133
 Appendix D: Social Deviance 135
 Appendix E: I Am 137
 Appendix E: My Purpose 159

List of Illustrations

The Human Spine 10
Standing Tall 11
My Brothers and Me 17
My Dad and Me 18
Being a Little Helper 18
Me, with Brace 22
My Daily Verses 57
Swimming Again! 61
Tracy and Me 63
Loving the Beach 65
Kayaking – No Chair! 69
Me, Standing Tall 70
Going Rafting 77
Tracy and Me on the Beach 89
Standing in the Exo Suit 95
Standing with my KAFO Braces 98
In My Standing Frame 99
Getting My Braces On – By Myself 100
Thank You All 113
Hello, Wonderful World! 117

Foreword

"The day came when the risk to remain tight in a bud was more painful than the risk it took to blossom." Anais Nin

This is what I have had the privilege of witnessing with Shelly. This unfolding and blossoming into self. Shelly's life story as you will soon be reading appears to be an ongoing trajectory towards suffering and pain. I know first-hand how easy it is to hang onto what we know, even if what we know will eventually kill us. It is so easy to remain stuck in resentment, shame, blame, hostility, and a frozen state of fear.

The journey Shelly shares here is that of the victim to the survivor. In this journey, she cultivates self-awareness and a love for life, a gratitude so enormous it has nowhere else to go but to heal the heart. When there is spaciousness enough to hold both accountability and fierce kindness, courage and vulnerability, boundaries and intimacy, this is what healing looks like. In a person that has been violated and has in turn violated themselves with addiction and self-loathing, this is what the grace of God looks like in a person. It looks like Shelly Kerchner.

You will be blessed beyond measure in reading this story and I pray you find something here that can give you hope. I am blessed beyond measure by Shelly, her light, her willingness to share and serve. May all beings be well. May all be free and safe from harm. May all have peace. Namaste.

Rachel Allen
Healing Arts Practitioner. CMP, E-RYT 200, Reiki Master/Teacher

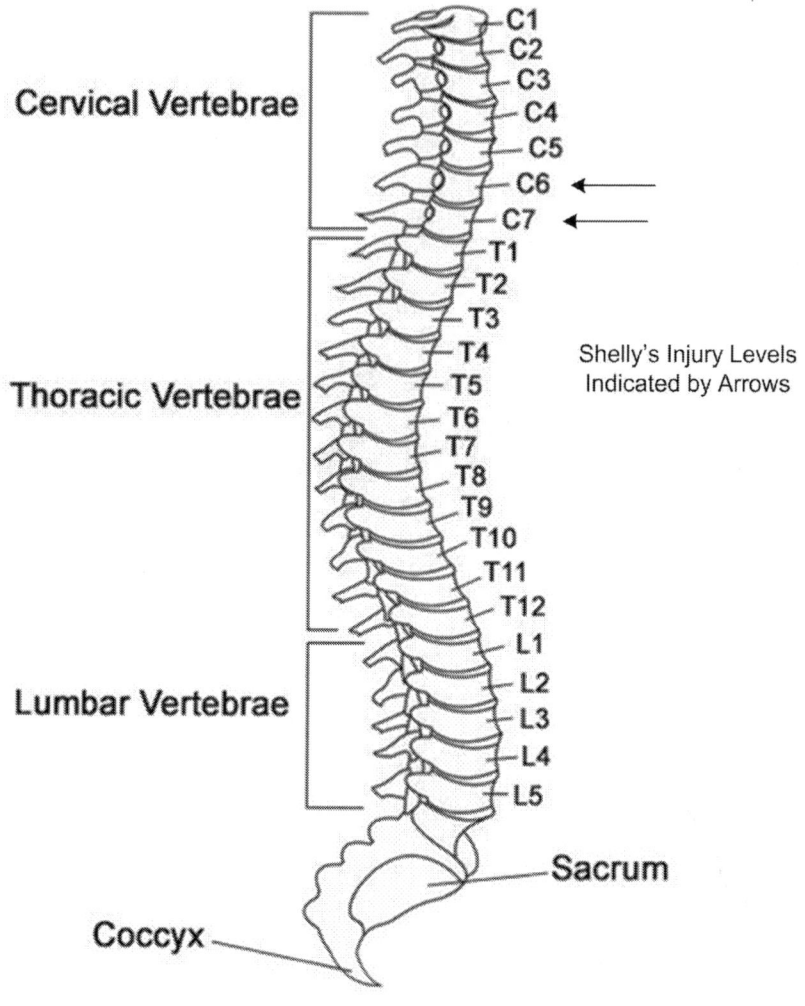

The Human Spine

CT scan of the cervical spine showed fractures through C6 resulting in a grade 4 anterolisthesis of C6 on C7 and narrowing of the central canal. CT scan of the thoracic spine showed scoliosis without fractures. The patient was taken to the operating room and underwent C6 through C7 anterior cervical discectomy with fusion at C5 through 6 and C3 through 7 with allograft in anterior plate with posterior fusion of C5 to C7 by Dr. Reiter.

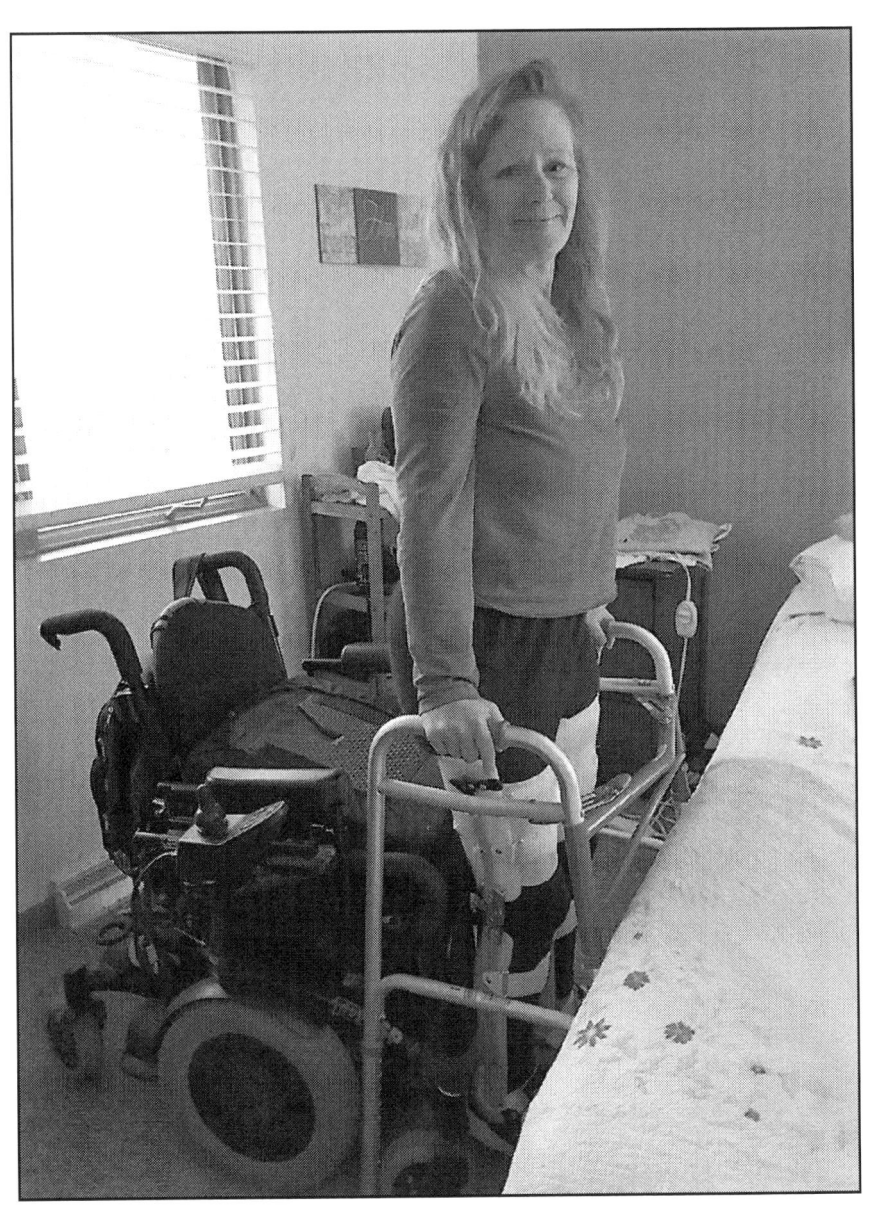

Standing Tall

Chapter 1. *My Purpose*

My purpose for writing this book is twofold: First, so that I have it as a tool to go back to when I stumble off the path of being grateful, and second, so others will have it for the same reason. I didn't know until my accident, but now I do, that gratitude is always attainable if I purposefully force myself to think correctly. Nothing worthwhile ever comes easily for me, and the art of gratitude was a hard lesson to learn. Immediate gratification is one of my downfalls, which is why I continued destructive behaviors chasing something outside of myself to fill that hole. The important thing is: I've learned it. I had lots of emptiness and needs that went unfilled as a child and I accept that.

Today it's my job to give myself all those things I needed and never got as a child. I was never shown how to love and nurture myself, so that will be my goal for the rest of my years. That form of peace of mind and security has never been found in a drink or drug and no one else can give it to me except me and my God of my understanding. When I'm at my best spiritually I can say if I'm supposed to have something God will see that it comes to pass. So, whatever happens, I am OK where I'm at. Whatever happens makes no difference to me!

I'm living a life free from bondage of self and of anything that alters my state of mind. Today I am responsible for myself and there is nothing in this world that can seriously hurt or upset me. I have boundaries to protect me from you and you from me. I'm free and living a life I've never dreamed possible, and for that I am grateful.

> *I'm free and living a life I've never dreamed possible, and for that I am grateful.*

I have my moments and frustrations with people and even loved ones, but I know in my heart we're all doing the best we can do from our level of understanding, and we do want the same things: to love and to be loved.

Everything that happens to a child of God is Father-filtered, and He intends it for good.

Life is what we make it: Double trauma meant double gratitude for me.

For those of us who have survived a traumatic experience, life takes on a whole new meaning. I have been transformed spiritually, emotionally, and physically. Each day I wake with a stronger sense of Grace and optimism I never knew existed.

Gratitude has become a part of me, and is intertwined in everything I do, think and say. It is no longer something I must try and grasp or chase after, because it is who I am. When sadness or disappointment creeps in I now can stop it in its tracks by reflecting to the day when I was paralyzed and was told I would never use my hands.

> *I may be paralyzed, but today I am free to be exactly the person God wants me to be.*

Losing control of my body forced me to control the only thing I could, and that was my thoughts. I never dealt with depression after my paralysis because I had a bonus of another trauma that was removed the day of my accident. I was removed from my abusive marriage, so when things got tough I said to myself, "It could be worse. I could still be stuck in my house and living under all that tension and dysfunction. I may be paralyzed, but today I am free to be exactly the person God wants me to be, not who my abuser wanted me to be."

I had to lose everything to appreciate the little things in life, and the result is that it doesn't take much for me to be happy. I can still remember what it was like not being able to lift an empty cup, cough independently, or even bend my fingers at will. The biggest gift of all was losing my mobility and then having all these little things slowly restored to me, along with a deeper sense of gratitude.

There is freedom in losing it all and escaping death, because today I have the gift of Grace and optimism to overcome anything. By losing it all, I now have access to unlimited grace, hope, and a personal strength unlike before. My purpose has been renewed and life today is all about uncovering, discovering, and discarding.

Every time I am asked to speak I heal a little more. Sometimes when I think I have grown all I can something else happens and I am in my cycle of accepting, adjusting, and moving on with a greater understanding of gratitude and peace.

There are times when doubt and fear slowly show up when I am asked to speak. Immediately, I am reminded to do it while afraid and not to be ashamed of my story because it may inspire others. Functioning in this manner keeps me moving forward, and if just one person is helped, that makes it all worthwhile!

The more I write down what I am grateful for, the more things I find to be grateful for.

Chapter 2. *Where I Came From*

From the outside, we looked like the perfect catholic family. Growing up, my brothers and I had all the material things children could want. There was an in-ground pool in our backyard with both a sliding and diving board, so it was the perfect place for my parents to entertain.

My Brothers and Me

Our house was always filled with family or friends of my parents. My father owned a car dealership specializing in Cadillacs, so his friends became the local doctors, lawyers, and politicians who all frequented our house for the parties and all the free booze you could drink.

The outcome of the parties was always negative, and ended with my parents fighting. As young as four I witnessed the violent arguments, and would sob while begging them to stop. To this day I still don't know where my brothers were and wonder why they never came out to try and make it stop.

My Dad and Me

As a young child I felt lost and alone, and I quietly asked God why he was punishing me. Surrounded by toys and all a child could want never made up for the attention I sought! My actions were summoning. I spent my days escaping in nature, making mud pies and climbing trees.

Being a Little Helper

My parents would drink, and the abuse began, and left me feeling like I had lost even before I had a chance. At the age of four I thought this chaos was normal. From that day on the bed wetting began. Growing up in an alcoholic home can feel like you are finished even before you start. The intense family shame breeds silence, and the result was for me to remain quiet. Longing for a connection, attention, and looking for direction became a part of everything I did.

My mom and I left when I was 12 and moved in with her new love. There was no more fighting, but my character had already taken form. My bedwetting came to a stop except when I drank too much. My brothers had introduced me to wine, and from day one I drank alcoholically, finishing a whole bottle by myself. It made me sick, and I blamed it on the wine, so I switched to beer and liquor.

To survive, I continued to deny all that I felt, and functioned the way I had been taught. I was only 13 years old, and feeling lost and alone, with no way to cope. It just seemed like a way of life.

I still recall the day my brothers introduced me to alcohol. For a short time, I felt like I had it all. Keep in mind this all seemed normal. From the first drink I drank, the cycle of addiction had me in its grip. With Dad's approval that we could indulge, I stopped my questioning "is this normal?"

Growing up in dysfunction is no way for a child to thrive. For by this time, my parent's dysfunction was ingrained in me. It was never God's intention that I be plagued by the thought of what was wrong with me, operating in so much fear and tension.

Over the years, I have had so many fears, and keeping things inside is no way to live. Drinking offered escape from life, which seemed like a nightmare filled with dysfunction of every type. There was too much drinking, fighting, and all the neglect that left me with all these feelings I didn't want to own. I just knew I would always be alone. Operating on emotion and overwhelmed by fears left me asking "is this all there is?"

> *But we only thought we had it all.*

In the garage, there were mini bikes and go carts, one for each of us. When we turned 16 each of us was given our own car. Our basement was filled with pinball machines, a pool table, slot machines, and all the board games a child could want. Dad even installed a barre for me so I could practice my ballet in the basement. But we only thought that we had it all.

All the material things never made up for the emotional emptiness that I felt. I longed to be connected to someone and to be a part of a greater good. For a short time my dear Kate helped me escape. She helped my Dad with the house, and babysat me long before my drinking began. She was the only thing constant in my life and with her I had one night a week of escape.

She was the Grandma I never had and had some insight to what was happening inside me. She was just the gentlest individual I have ever met. I know she did what she could to help me straighten my path. Time with her gave me hope that someday I could have a happy life. Every Thursday night we watched the Walton's and for a short time I found escape and dreamed about how wonderful it would be to have a family such as that.

Kate was the one to discover things no one else could, and knew more about me than my own mother ever could. Kate was the one who discovered my bed wetting when I was six. I overheard Kate telling my mom one morning that she once again found my sheets soaked with urine. Looking back, I still remember how terrified I was. I felt a twang of guilt and was fearful of how my mother would react.

Mom never approached me and we both pretended the problem didn't exist. Her silence was to me an admission of her disappointment in me. I drew my own conclusions about what she thought and none of it was positive. I was so young, fragile, afraid, and full of shame to even approach her about it. Secretly, I was longing for Mom to take me in her arms and tell me it was OK. That reassurance never came, and I was left feeling alone and even more insecure. And for years I remained silent because of my embarrassment.

I remember being a little angry on one occasion. Our house was full of company, as it often was. I was in my room with the door closed while sitting on the floor. I was holding a rosary and crying. In frustration, I tore the rosary and threw it across my room. I was angry at God and questioning why was I being punished like this. Being angry at God is no way to live, and I hated Him. The dysfunction and denial continued along with my bed wetting. I was ashamed and had no one to talk to.

Inside our house there was alcoholism, domestic violence, and verbal and emotional abuse. Amidst the constant chaos and uncertainty, we suffered as a family and individually. The dysfunction continued until finally my mom tried one last effort to save our family and made an appointment for us to see a family therapist. We attended one session and never returned.

My Grandmother was diagnosed with terminal cancer and Mom spent the next six months caring for her until she passed. My grandparents owned a bar, so when she was finished caring for her mom she would tend the bar. Mom's drinking only progressed and she went days without coming home, never sleeping in her bed.

As a kid I saw so many things I shouldn't have and was spending way too much time at our family bar. I understand now why my mom drank. She grew up in an alcoholic home filled with dysfunction. Her father shook when denied a drink and when I asked "why?" I was told a lie.

Shame took root in my family years before I was born. My mother's mom was cold and distant and not showing emotion because of not knowing how to show any affection. Mom did the best she could with what she knew and decided she deserved to start anew. I love my mom and know she did the best she could do.

My mom grew up without hearing the words "I love you" and was never hugged, so she made sure we had lots of hugs and heard "I love you" a lot. Talking about feelings was not done in her house, so obviously she could not transmit what she hasn't got. She did try to give us what she never had and I love her for that.

At this point I was in the fifth grade and I was diagnosed with scoliosis. For the next four years, I was expected to wear a Milwaukee brace 23 hours a day, made from metal and leather. I continued to wet the bed and would wake up and the leather around my pelvic area would be soaked with urine and I would say nothing; I would just wear the brace anyway. It was extremely uncomfortable and heavy and made my summers unbearable. It was horrible being surrounded by leather and metal.

Me, with Brace

My pelvis and buttocks area were covered by a pelvic leather shell that buckled in the back, making it impossible to for me to put it on or take it off without help. The metal bar extended from my pelvis area to underneath my jaw where my chin rested. This restricted any movement in my neck area. The two bars in the rear started at my hair line and were attached to the pelvic shell. It was impossible to turn to the right or left without moving my entire body.

There was a strap that was positioned on my right side and one on the left that attached to the metal bar in the front and the two bars in the back. The goal was to straighten my spine with the help of those straps. Quietly I suffered and wondered why God was doing this to me.

I hated Him. I was angry inside, stuffed my feelings, and just wore the brace. I don't remember having any conversations with anyone about how I felt about this; I just did what I had to do. My dad felt horrible for me and would have worn the brace for me if it was possible. He hurt and I hurt but I needed to be strong for him.

He knew he was losing his wife and wanted desperately for her to be there for me. We would get late night angry phone calls from the wife of my mom's lover telling Dad to get his wife under control. My heart ached for him while he felt sorry for me. He would kneel by my bed at times and just sob while I did the best I could to console him.

> *He would kneel by my bed at times and just sob while I did the best I could to console him.*

All I wanted was to be reassured. That assurance never came from anyone around me, so I continued the facade of being OK when inside I was dying and angry at God for punishing us like this. To deal with it I started to shoplift, even though I had no reason to. I just was addicted to what it did to my brain. When I stole something, I experienced a rush of "good" feelings. I never got caught, but I did this for several months and don't recall experiencing any type of escape again until I took my first drink.

I lived in a constant state of fear and insecurity before I got my Milwaukee brace and now that insecurity and fear was compounded by my medical diagnosis. Looking back now, I dealt with it by portraying a strong exterior, kept a smile on my face, and tried to be the one who was going to make everything OK. That job was assigned to me the day I was born, and I tried to fill those shoes throughout my entire life.

I was introduced to alcohol by my brothers at age 13 and drank to get drunk from day one. Drinking temporarily stopped the hurt and numbed all the pain I was experiencing, and thus the cycle of addiction began. My parents divorced and Mom and I left. Once I was out of the toxic environment, my bed wetting stopped. My brothers stayed with my father.

It was an adjustment for me, because I was pulled out of Catholic school and sent to public. I spent weekends and Wednesday night with my dad and brothers. Dad permitted drinking if we stayed at the house, so I spent a lot of time at his place. My mom had no idea what was happening at Dad's since there was no form of communication between them.

This continued for several years, and I gained 50 pounds from booze and wanted to lose weight. I became obsessed with losing weight and the more weight I lost the more compliments I got. I swapped one addiction for another and my battle with anorexia began. The constant turmoil I was enduring throughout my life made itself evident in my eating disorder. Everything around me was out of my control except restricting my food intake. My weight dropped to 89 pounds.

Chapter 3. *Anorexia and Alcohol*

At this same time, I was experiencing episodes of an overwhelming sensation that I had been here and/or done this before. My stomach would turn and I would panic and just become overwhelmed with a feeling I wanted to flee from wherever I was. It was the scariest feeling in the world and no one could figure out what was wrong with me.

I was misdiagnosed for five years and was in and out of psych wards. The diagnosis was that I suffered from panic attacks and a mental disorder. At the age of sixteen I was afraid, feeling alone, and still desperately seeking something constant in my life. I needed something that I could hold onto; just wanted some label to help me be able to identify and possibly correct the path that was laid out before me.

My parents could not help me and the doctors gave up on me. I learned to cope and ease my pain the best way I could and my anorexia got worse. I was admitted to the eating disorder clinic at Johns Hopkins's Hospital. I was glad to be away from my dysfunctional family and I was also hopeful they would find a solution to my "panic attacks." The nurses and doctors were great, and finally someone was taking care and paying attention to me. For the first time in my life I was experiencing security. I was assigned a primary and secondary nurse upon the day of admission who monitored my progress or lack thereof.

A goal weight was determined and the dietitian designed a proper meal plan to achieve that goal weight. There were a total of 10 girls on the floor with me. Competition was evident among us in regards to who was the thinnest and a hierarchy was formed on that basis.

Georgia was my roommate and we bonded immediately, because our stories were similar in nature and both shared a common background of family dysfunction.

The thinnest girl was granted respect and was looked up to. With her gray skin tone, fine body hair growth, sunken eyes, and slow motor movements, society would label Grace as weak and frail. But to us she was a representation of strength, stability, and security. Her intravenous (IV) was a symbol of power, authority, and incredible display of self-discipline and control that all of us longed to have and were willing to die for.

Mealtimes lasted one hour, and anyone who was remaining at the table after the allotted time was escorted to seclusion until her meal was consumed. After meal times there was supervision for a total of two hours to prevent elimination of food. This time was diminished as we gained weight.

If anyone needed to use the restroom, we were escorted and required to keep the bathroom door ajar. We were monitored at night to prevent excess exercising. Every morning the team of doctors and nurses would make rounds and evaluate our progress.

We felt special, and for once in our lives someone was taking care of us. Some of the girls gained enough weight to be released, but immediately would return to starvation or change addictions. I did the latter.

> *Grace was defiant and that defiance ultimately took her life.*

Recovery from my eating disorder meant no longer having control, thus the reason for the switch from one destructive behavior to another or swapping anorexia for bulimia or vice versa. Grace was defiant and that defiance ultimately took her life.

In a few months, I reached my goal weight of 104 and was discharged. The doctors never did properly diagnose my "panic attacks" and they continued daily. I was having as many as 14 per day.

There was no support group for anorexics so it was recommended that I attend Over Eaters Anonymous because we were all dealing with the same demons, but only used different ways to numb our pain. I attended my first OA meeting and was told I belonged in AA. Bewildered, I followed their advice.

I was 18 and finally ended up in rehab at Mount Manor in Emmetsburg, PA. My stay was short because of my various disorders, and they were not equipped to treat them, so instead I was admitted to the Meadows where my eating and drinking additions were addressed. I was finally sober, but still was experiencing "panic attacks" and when released it was under the agreement that I would live with my aunt where the dysfunction and alcohol abuse was not as prevalent. I was again sent home without a proper diagnosis for my "attacks" but agreed to attend ninety meetings in ninety days and continuing to find a new path.

I attended AA and got involved in service. After two years of sobriety I was sharing my story of recovery at local hospitals. A gentleman approached me afterwards and suggested that I go to see a doctor friend of his because what I was describing did not sound like a mental condition to him. Instead, he suspected that it was physical. I saw the doctor, and went through all the scans. The doctor knew right away what was stopping me from finding my way.

I was diagnosed with having a Right Mesial Temporal brain tumor, which was causing seizures, while the panic and odd sensation I was experiencing was an aura before a seizure. The tumor was removed and my seizures decreased to one a year. I was happy for the first time in my life, and no longer full of fear!

I thanked God for all of my blessings and for removing my thoughts of "maybe I AM crazy". Thanks to AA and my new family there my life started once again. I was no longer alone and no longer hated God, but instead sought him out with all I've got. The answer became clear -- life would be OK if I stayed clear of alcohol. Thanks to Alcoholics Anonymous I had found answers to my problems and finally was hopeful of all the things that had yet to come.

Chapter 4. *Troubled Love*

I was sober the first time for seven years. AA helped me get the God thing straightened out and I no longer saw Him as a punishing God. It was suggested to me that I use the group as "a power greater than me," and I could do that. I could not deny the existence of God, because I witnessed changes in people and in my own life that were unexplainable.

Whenever I walked into a meeting, the feeling of being alone vanished and for the first time in my life felt like I belonged. There was a joy and a peace that the members possessed, and I wanted that, and had to find a way to make it my own. Life was good, and for once in my life I was right where I was supposed to be. Because of the 12 steps, I could see where I went wrong, and how the decisions I made only hurt me. I forgave my parents and knew in my heart they both did the best that they could. They were doing only what they were taught to do.

Against my sponsor's advice, after a few years of sobriety, I started dating a man in AA. He was caring and kind and offered me hope, protection, and security that I thought I would never find. I was vulnerable, and thought I was in love.

Today I understand that vulnerability was used to gain my trust, and methodically and ultimately he isolated me by convincing me that my family was not safe for me to be around. He told me that he believed my parents loved me but they did not know how to care for me.

I conceded that he was correct, and slowly he won my confidence. However, the emotional abuse and conditioning was pervasive and was designed to keep me constantly off balance and in a state of self-doubt.

Eventually we both started drinking. For the next 16 years, we were both caught up in the cycle of addiction. As my drinking progressed I stopped taking care of myself and stopped taking my seizure medication because he posed the question, "How do you know if you really need it if you never stop taking it? It honestly seemed logical to me at the time.

The isolation from my family was slow, and ultimately I was not around them unless he was with me. After being isolated from family and friends I felt stuck, but I was too weak to walk away. I was not the person God intended me to be and was empty inside, which led to even more drinking.

I did not leave the house without my husband knowing about it, and then was expected to call him at work to let him know I was home. He didn't like me going away with my mom or even talking to her, because he didn't want her inside my head. In his opinion, she was a bad influence on me, and he would say that if she knew anything about being married she still would be.

The only way I saw her was if we both went. That way he could control our relationship. Friends would ask me to get together, and I knew he would not approve, so I would lie and say I can't or didn't want to. Eventually they stopped asking.

He trusted no one, including his own mother. If I talked to her he wanted to know exactly what we talked about, who else was there and how long I was there. I got tired of getting drilled if I left the house so I slowly stopped going out except to go to the grocery store, church, or for a run at the track. Those three things only involved calling before I left and then again when I got home. I did not have to answer as many questions for any of those.

I started to attend daily Mass to get out of the house. I was looking for God's love, protection, and care, and coming up empty handed.

Then one night I was flipping through channels and saw Joyce Meyer. She was secure and confident and I wanted to possess that. She claimed the way to find God's confidence was to find out who God says I am. I watched her every chance I got, but had to sneak so I would not get caught. I knew he would not approve.

It's clear to me today how God was empowering me with the tools necessary for me to persevere, heal, and continue fighting to regain some semblance of independence.

Unknown to me was that in a few short months, I would be literally fighting for my life.

Appreciate the little things in life because someday you will look back and realize they were the big things.

Chapter 5. *The End, and the Beginning*

July 31 2006, I woke up, packed my husband's lunch, saw him off to work, and was anxious to go for my three-mile run on such a beautiful summer day. After returning home, I sat down to eat and experienced an aura and I panicked. I rushed out my front door to get help. Instead of going down two steps I took a left and tumbled into my garden and fell and hit my head.

My neighbor saw me fall and called 911. I was still conscious and had no pain, so I did not panic until she informed me that the ambulance was on its way. My first thought was "Oh my God I must lock the door or I am going to get in trouble."

I repeatedly tried to get up by propping myself up on my elbows but kept failing. She insisted that I stay still to minimize the injury, so when I realized I was not going to get up, in desperation I asked her to go in inside, get my pocketbook, and make sure to lock the door. She did just that and was by my side until the ambulance arrived.

The next memory I have was looking at the EMT's and asking if I was ever going to be able to move my legs. He stared at me and said "I don't know." My clothing was cut off of me and X-rays were taken. He returned saying that he had bad news and I had fractured my spine. The ER doctor took X-rays and told me "I have bad news. You fractured your spine at C6-C7."

I did not comprehend the severity of what just happened to me and what it all meant for my future. Never again would I feel the awesomeness of my feet touching the earth, my toes in the sand, or what it feels like to run. Life as I knew it would never be the same.

They prepared me to be flown to Hershey Medical Center. Next I remember the sound of the Life Line helicopter. It was by far the loudest noise I had ever heard.

I was in and out of consciousness at this point. We landed within 20 minutes and I was prepared for emergency surgery. I was sedated while lying prone on the table and drifted between consciousness and unconsciousness. I was sedated but still could hear the doctor say "She is such a pretty girl."

Everything else just disappeared. I was lying on a mat table for days listening to everything that was said. I was told, "You are never going to get out of this bed or even lift your head."

> *For weeks, I was floating in another world, somewhere between life and death, stuck in a place of rest.*

My eyes were closed but still I saw, and I heard it all after my fall. I was told I had lost it all. Surrounded by strength and saved by grace and gratitude became my sacred place. For weeks, I was floating in another world, somewhere between life and death, stuck in a place of rest. My eyes were opened and I slowly realized all I ever needed and dreamed of is right here inside. That ultimate power was always available, and was with me all along. My searching would soon cease.

The greatest gift I learned after my fall is that the secret to success is sharing and is the only way to have it all. I'm now committed to doing good, passing it on whenever hope calls. I do it despite my fear and always am rewarded by having fewer tears. Only God knows what's in store for me next and whatever that is, I will still feel very blessed!

Everything went black. I was on life support and a feeding tube for days and my family was told my chances to survive were slim to none. It was difficult for my mom because the doctor would only talk to Gary and he did not share much info with my parents.

I do have a memory of being in a cold, dark room and lying on a mat table with tubes coming from everywhere. There was a metal device holding my head and neck area still. The nurse would sit and talk to me for hours at a time. I was not capable of any movement and speaking was impossible. The only thing I can remember about those two weeks was hearing the nurse say, "You are just going to have to accept the fact that you will never be able to walk."

I was fighting for my life, and cannot describe the helplessness I felt. The next two weeks I was incoherent, and was not expected to survive. I recall after being intubated for the second time, my husband was by my side asking me if I wanted to stay where I was or go to another hospital. I was scared and said to "hear" not realizing what I was signing up to do.

Gary was controlling the flow of information to my parents and making decisions for me. Looking back now, if I had had all my faculties, I would have insisted that I go to a rehab specializing in spinal cord injury. Unfortunately, that was not possible, because I was still under the control of my husband who now had the power to make the decisions. He was not, in fact, thinking what was best for me, so that never came to be.

I think he saw only more cost, so did not push for me to get proper treatment. This very fact still motivates me today, because I think of the possibilities and what could have been. Yesterday is gone and I have moved on. Today my goal is to continue to heal and work on reactivating my dormant muscles. My fate is in God's hands, and as long as I keep working and forging ahead on improving, the possibilities are endless.

> *My fate is in God's hands, and as long as I keep working and forging ahead on improving, the possibilities are endless.*

God had other plans for my life that fateful day, because finally I woke up, came off the ventilator, and was happy to be alive. I remember that day like it was yesterday, and still recall the gratitude I felt in my heart. I was just so thankful that I could open my eyes and was able to see daylight. I was no longer in the dark and cold room.

Directly in front of me were Mom, Dad, and my brother Scott. They were they first people I saw. I was wearing a Miami J collar around my neck for stabilization, which only intensified my feeling of being paralyzed. I was surrounded by pillows to keep me from falling to either side and was confined even more because of being paralyzed.

Then I slowly realized that I was unable to move from my neck down. I slowly opened my eyes and was joyful inside. I could feel my family staring at me and when my eyes met theirs I smiled hoping it would ease their concern. My mom looked so sad and scared, and I just wanted to ease her pain.

It did not matter to me that I was unable to move from my neck down. I knew they needed me at this moment to be strong so we all could rebound. I was still alive, thankful to be out of the dark, and so anxious to make a new start. This day made me look at life in such a whole new light.

Chapter 6. *Manifestation of Power*

PT (Physical Therapy) and OT (Occupational Therapy) technicians came to work with me in surgical intensive care, and immediately began moving my arms for me.

My next taste of freedom came when my neck collar came off! My neck was tender and forced me to only make gentle movements for the next few weeks.

For a short while, I was spoon fed by a nurse and eventually learned how to feed myself using adaptive silverware that fit on my wrist. Accomplishing the basic task of hitting my mouth and not my chin was exhilarating, and left me with a longing to gain more independence.

My next accomplishment was my PT and OT moving me into a chair. I had no trunk control and no hand function but it was another proud moment!

One morning I was lying in bed staring at my hand when the doctor visited and he commented, "You are never going to be able to use your hands." I didn't respond to him because my body was telling me something different. My hand was not visibly moving but inside I felt my muscles were trying to flex.

SCI (Spinal Cord Injury) is not a textbook diagnosis, and recovery is different for everyone. The nurses told me that it was a joy to have me on their floor and said "We are not used to making arrangements for patients to leave this floor, because when they come here it's to die." It truly is a miracle that I am alive today, and I am thankful God gave me a second chance at life.

Eventually I was moved to a normal room. Then, while receiving a breathing treatment, my left lung collapsed. I panicked and while gasping for air I remember thinking that after all I this, I was going to die, and everything went black. My family didn't know if they would ever get me back. I was once again put on a ventilator. And again my family was told that I had a small chance of coming off it a second time.

Thankfully, I woke up a few days later, again with a rush of gratitude that had doubled from before. This feeling was so foreign and rare that I still feel the impact today. It is a feeling that I have tried to bottle up and hold onto because it's just like nothing I had ever experienced before.

From this point on, I promised myself that as soon as I was mobile I would find a computer and search for prayers. In a few days, I was moved again, and I asked to see a priest. He did come to see me but it was an uncomfortable exchange. It was like he did not know what to say to me so his visit was short, and he never returned.

> *I made a decision to focus on the things that were going right and give physical therapy my all.*

My husband was not there much, and I was grateful to be away from him. I needed to hear from God, so I tried saying Our Fathers and Hail Marys but they were no longer working. I needed something more. The cards started coming in and I hung on to these words to keep me going. "Everything that happens to a child of God is Father-filtered, and He intends to use it for good." I made a decision to focus on the things that were going right and give physical therapy my all.

The day finally came when I could transfer to a chair without the help of two people, and gained enough trunk control to sit upright for a few seconds without falling over. For weeks, they would help me onto the mat at PT and I would fall directly over. My muscles were still extremely weak and still lacked hand function, and had no fine motor skills. I relied on my wrists to wheel myself to a computer and typed using a device that attached to my wrist. I found a prayer that day that changed my life.

> *"Thank you Father for all that you have given me. Thank you Father for all that you have taken from me and thank you Father for all that you have left me."*

My struggle lessened as my gratitude grew. I had a great nurse who had over 20 years of experience working with SCI patients, and immediately I trusted her. Nancy had confidence in my ability to accomplish my goals. She showed me how to use my tenodesis grip to try and pick things up.

The tenodesis effect is that when you bend your wrist upwards, it tends to curl your fingers and bring your thumb closer to your hand, and when relaxed, your fingers open.

Because of her, I never stopped trying to use my hands. One morning Nancy walked into my room and announced, "Today we are going to learn how to cath in bed." From that day on I found out all about catheterization.

Up until now the nurses were taking care of all that. I learned how to cath myself using my tenodesis and a mirror between my legs. It was difficult, but I did it and that made me happy.

I met one patient who had no function at all, and used a mouth stick to operate his chair. Seeing him made me realize how much I had to be grateful for, and that no matter what I am going through, there are always those who have it so much worse.

> *Seeing him made me realize how much I had to be grateful for, and that no matter what I am going through, there are always those who have it so much worse.*

Chapter 7. *Pitiful to Powerful*

My transformation from being pitiful to powerful was just beginning, and my healing process now was inevitable.

My nurse Nancy was the first to pick up on how badly my husband was treating me. I dreaded his visits because he would constantly make statements like, "I want to know who is inside your head and who you are talking to." He wanted to know what nurses were taking care of me and wanted a full report on what they did to me and exactly what I did during the day.

When Gary found out that there was a male nurse on my floor he became angry and said, "I do not want his hands on you." Frustrated, I said "My God, Gary, you are sick; he is a nurse and is just doing his job. What is wrong with you?"

The exchanges between us usually ended abruptly because of the individuals coming in and out of my room. But from that day on, if I had the male nurse I didn't tell Gary. I was so happy when our visits would come to an end.

Gary was used to knowing what I did before I did it and now that it was not the case he was becoming increasing hostile. No longer was I isolated at home where I could be controlled.

He turned sarcastic in a family meeting when my doctors and care team asked how he was doing he replied, "Oh, besides being spiritually, financially, and emotionally bankrupt I guess OK." He was no longer in control of me and it was clear he was becoming increasingly angry with me. He would call and by the time I hung up I was in tears.

One call came just as my PT and OT were entering my room for a session on how to dress myself in bed. I told him I had to get going and his response was "Oh yeah, well, they are more important than me." I was so angry I slammed the phone down.

I understood his life was changed the day of my accident, but it was becoming increasingly apparent he was not concerned with how I was doing. Never did he ask if I was OK. He was only thinking about himself and getting his own needs met.

After sixteen years of taking care of him, I was going to take care of myself, and prove to myself I was not helpless like he believed. This was my opportunity to find out who I was without him there to monitor and control everything around me. My accident was a blessing in disguise because it got me away from him.

Nancy taped one of my last sessions of getting dressed in the hopes that my husband would watch it and then have empathy of what I was going through, and to get a taste of what my life was going to be like. He never had the desire to watch the tape but I did, and I finally saw what was blocking me from accomplishing my task of pulling my pants up in bed.

The answer was to put the head of the bed down far enough that I could rock backwards to gain enough momentum to pull one leg onto the other so I could put my leg into the pant leg. What a happy day!

The nurses were so encouraging, and applauded when I would accomplish something for the first time. After the nurse helped me transfer out of bed I would stay in my chair for the rest of the day, being vigilant about performing the proper amount of weight shifts to guard against sores.

Normal people just move when their body signals that it's time to. Since my muscles were compromised from my injury, I need to make weight shifts a normal part of my daily routine.

> *On a daily basis I learned how to make a big deal of the so-called little things, and still to this day celebrate the "small things"; it's what brings me happiness.*

My physical therapist wanted me to move more in my wheelchair, and at first this seemed like an insurmountable task. I had no grip, so I used my wrists to push my chair, and because I was so weak I only moved from my bed to the door on my first try, only moving an inch at a time.

I had a lot of time after PT and OT, so this was how I spent my time. I kept a smile on my face and was determined to make it the past the door the next time, and so on, until I finally made it the whole way around the first floor and ended up where I began. I did accomplish this goal before I left!

I was shown different ways to accomplish basic tasks that most people take for granted, by getting creative and consistently trying to use my quadriplegic hands. I had to learn to utilize what function I had left. Getting wheelchair gloves on and pinching and pulling was impossible until I was shown how to use my teeth.

Then I discovered that I could snap my bra by utilizing my teeth. I clenched it between my teeth while they propped me up in front of my sink. I found things were easier when I could see what I was doing. In time, I could snap my bra using my mouth, both hands, and the mirror. After it was snapped I just pulled it over my head and my mission was complete.

Even today there is always a way to do something; I just have to be creative enough to figure one out. My OT gave me an adaptive brush that had a strap attached to it so I could fix my own hair. However I still could not pull my hair back in a ponytail, so the nurse did it for me one morning. She left and Nancy stopped to see me and I was not myself. She asked what was wrong and I said between tears, "I am so sick and tired of not being able to do my own hair."

That was the first time I expressed sadness, shedding a few tears, and she was glad that I finally cried. Up until that day I tried to and just couldn't.

It did make me wonder why. There was only one other SCI patient there, and when it was quiet I could hear him yelling profanities at the nurses. My doctor asked if I could stop and talk to him while I passed his room, and I did, but was never certain if my visit helped him. I know his pain was real and he needed some time. I spoke to Nancy about it and she said not to take it personally, and that they understand.

I continued to wonder quietly if something was wrong with me because my lack of tears and all negative emotion. My early childhood training kicked in, I suppose. I was thankful to be out of my house, away from the abuse, and dwelled on what made me feel good.

Learning everything all over again and accomplishing each task left me searching for ways to gain more freedom back. Strangely to me, my accident started to seem like a blessing in disguise because I was no longer stuck in a marriage I couldn't leave. I was thankful I was no longer under the control of my husband. I didn't care so much about my lack of mobility because where I had been living was much worse than this.

When I was not sleeping, I dedicated my time to physical therapy. Because of the doctor's prognosis of only having a tenodesis grip with no expectation of any hand improvement, my rehab therapy was only physical and involved transfers and wheelchair mobility, and trying to maneuver on the mat table.

My PT expected success, so I pushed myself with an energy I didn't know I possessed. I struggled, but never did I think of giving up, and continued pushing toward success. I tried to do what she asked to the point of leaving my three month stay with a hernia in my abdomen. My husband was furious that they "sent me home with a hernia." Looking back now, the truth was he did not want me home period, because in his opinion I had turned into a burden.

Chapter 8. *Going Home*

My three months in rehab was up, and I needed to return home. There was a lot of planning to do and thinking about it made me blue. There was so much to do just to make that happen.

My brother built a ramp made in sections, which made transporting it from New York to Pennsylvania easier to do. Once that was finished, we had all the necessary equipment, such as a potty chair and a hospital bed, delivered to the house so it was ready for me to use.

Saying goodbye to the doctors and nurses was bittersweet. My doctor told me that I changed them and was a joy to have as a patient and he would remember me forevermore. He asked what my plans were, and I said I am still unsure.

He reiterated that I changed them and if I would get a degree in Social Work he would hire me. He gave me hope because I thought that was something I could do.

My mom and my husband showed up to take me home. He was very indignant and as he approached me he said, "Who were you saying goodbye to? Your girlfriend or boyfriend?" I felt fear and the tears started to flow.

I was afraid to go home now but it was too late. On the way home we stopped at the beer distributor and we started drinking while driving home.

My first night home was not good. We got drunk; he passed out and disappeared. Mom helped me transfer into bed. I still needed help with cathing and when I woke the next morning, I found myself trapped in bed until the VNA (Visiting Nurses Association) nurse came to the house.

He was still upstairs sleeping while I lay scared. The doorbell rang several times and I was terrified they would leave. Thankfully, the back door was unlocked and they entered that way. I was crying when they got there, but was so happy to see them because my bladder was so full I had no idea what to do.

That morning we figured out a daily schedule for the nurse's aide to visit and decided what ADL's (Activities for Daily Living) to help me with.

The scheduling nurse wanted a house key to make things easier on me. That did not go over well with Gary. He was opposed to the idea of them being there at all. Then when I protested he said "OK, they can come but I don't want them upstairs or down." He was making impossible demands, because the bathroom was upstairs and the laundry was downstairs, and to be of assistance to me they needed to access both areas.

As the days passed, he became increasingly angry with me and our lack of privacy. One morning before he left for work he asked indignantly, "How many keys do you want made?" He was clearly disturbed and pained to ask the question. I replied, "Look, either you need to care for me or you must let them come in, and obviously, you cannot."

Chapter 9. *Time to Leave*

It was at that moment I thought it might be time for me to leave. He glared at me and turned to leave for work. Finally I felt relief; some of the tension was gone.

At night, when we were alone, he continually made sarcastic comments such as, "You can forget about any dreams you may have, we had a good run while it lasted." Another one was "Handicapped people are not worth much but they sure are fun to watch."

The drunker he got the meaner his remarks became. The tension in the house could be felt by all who entered and it became increasingly apparent to me that I was not safe. Life as he knew it was over and his resentment towards me grew. For the next two weeks, the VNA was in and out of our house along with PT and OT.

There was a power struggle going on between Gary and me. He was losing control of me and again became verbally abusive and taunted me while I lay in bed helpless. He was talking and spitting in my face trying to get some type of a reaction from me. I remained quiet and just stared at the wall with no expression at all. Meanwhile, the taunting continued.

At that moment, I decided I had to get out of that house. My mother and I planned my escape and were unsuccessful our first few attempts. He always seemed to figure out that something was up, and delayed leaving for work. Then finally one day we were successful. After he left for work I called my mom to let her know all was clear. I did this despite of my fear. She and my nurse's aide carried me and my wheelchair out of that house. I left everything behind except my medical equipment and the clothes on my back. It did not matter, because I was away from him and was bound and determined to be transformed from pitiful to powerful.

Maybe the journey isn't about becoming anything. Maybe it's about unbecoming everything you were never supposed to be in the first place.

I was now living in my mom's two room school house. She had a restaurant on one side and lived in the other. She had a hospital bed set up for me in her kitchen. My physical therapy and OT started visiting at Mom's. Immediately after I was removed from my stressful living arrangement, and to my surprise, my healing accelerated. It was not evident to me until then how much stress prevents healing.

My OT Allison was the first therapist to focus on my hands, and started electrical stimulation therapy on my dominant hand. With only a tenodesis grip, I did not have much hope, but followed her instruction and did exactly what she asked.

> *I can still see her today intently looking and waiting to see some kind of muscle movement, and each time seeing no results.*

I had electrical stimulation therapy on just my right hand to force my muscles to contract. For weeks I would place my hands palm down on the table while thinking about the action of pressing down with each finger, holding that thought for 10 seconds, even though nothing visually was happening. Allison assured me that just thinking about it was good enough. I can still see her today intently looking and waiting to see some kind of muscle movement, and each time seeing no results.

I constantly worked with therapy putty, picked thousands of beads up and put them in empty soda bottles, and did my hand exercises with the hope of regaining my fine motor skills. Progress was painfully slow, but Allison never gave me an indication that there was no hope. She kept coming back and never gave up on me, so neither did I.

My first time in the shower required both my PT and OT to help, because I had no trunk control whatsoever. That made lifting my legs almost impossible. After I got onto the shower/tub bench, they helped with my legs. I could not hold myself up, so Audrey was behind me supporting my back and Allison was by my side. Once I was on the bench, they slid it over the tub and locked it in position.

It took about two arduous hours the first time and we were all exhausted afterwards. But I wanted my privacy, and that gave me the determination to learn how to do this by myself.

My mom was over-protective, and didn't like me taking chances. So instead of fighting with her, I would wait until she left the house, and then

I would practice transfers onto my tub bench and then take a shower. At the time it was so overwhelming, because you must constantly think about how to move next. Nothing was easy, and that made any accomplishment exhilarating! I was slow, but that did not matter. I realized after many close calls that slower is better sometimes.

My Physical Therapist Audrey was a mom with two teenage girls. She was very spiritual, and we bonded almost instantly. She was amazed at my positive attitude and asked what kept me going. I attributed it to my faith in God and my belief that all things work for good.

Audrey worked on my transfers, and eventually I was able to transfer into my mom's car. As soon as that goal was accomplished, I could start traveling to my PT appointments. Audrey's job would be complete. I was sad to lose her as my physical therapist but happy to gain a friend.

I started to attend Audrey's church and eventually became a member. The service was completely opposite of what I experienced in my catholic service. In the Brethren church, there is a sense of community, and I especially loved that we had an opportunity to share with the congregation our blessings, cares, or concerns.

Pastor Lyn came to visit at home to discuss my interest in joining the Brethren church. While sharing my story, I told her that I know God wants me to learn something from all this; I just don't know what it is yet. She said in a caring voice, "Maybe it's not all about you, Shelly". Wow, that makes sense! That's why people are reacting to me the way they are! I was so caught up in trying to figure God out that I neglected to see how He was using my situation to better help myself and others.

For example, one day after physical therapy I was outside waiting for my aide to pick me up, and a lady came up to me, handed me her orange juice, and said "You deserve this more than me" and then turned and walked away.

I was stunned and humbled at the same time. I had no idea she was watching me in PT. It was great to see real-time how God was working in both our lives! That experience made me realize that I needed to be careful of how I act and what I say, because I never know how God wants to use me and my situation to change others.

The next three months, whenever I was not in PT I was doing my hand therapy exercises at home. Bruce, my PT, confronted me one day after witnessing me getting out of my van. He pointed out that my aide was doing too much for me and mentioned this was her way of keeping her job security and he wanted me to change that.

I knew he was right; there was no reason I was not pushing my own wheelchair and at least trying to take my coat off. My aide was just doing her job and quickly jumped in to take care of me. I just let her help but in doing that I was cheating myself.

I am grateful to him for bringing that to my attention and voicing his concerns, because it was time I started to stand up for myself. I started insisting that my aides and my mom let me do more for myself. Hesitantly they agreed, but it took a long time for them to get used to my new rule. I told them that I know they want to help me, and I promised if I needed their help I would ask.

I needed to try and do things even though I was slow and clumsy! It felt great asserting myself and coming to the realization that doing some things quicker is not always better! I kept a journal of every single accomplishment no matter how small. (Appendix B)

In my opinion, my drinking began to interfere with my healing. I spoke to my mom and voiced my concern for both of us. She agreed but did not see the need for her to change. I knew it was time for me to change so instead of drinking I started researching who I was in Christ and wrote it all out on paper. I spent hours doing this.

There were a lot of "feelings" I needed to sort through and also needed to find out who I was and not who my husband said I was. I was slowly getting my independence back, and was on cloud nine. With my journal I kept track of things like the first time I was able to open up a packet of oatmeal without my adaptive scissors. I can tell you the day I was finally able to wheel to the sink, turn on the water, and put toothpaste onto my tooth brush.

Accomplishing all these tasks made life worth living and made me as happy as could be. Those moments of gratitude and thankfulness kept me moving forward and wanting more. I was constantly celebrating my accomplishments, and being grateful, and making a big deal of the little things in life that kept me going.

> *I was constantly celebrating my accomplishments, and being grateful, and making a big deal of the little things in life that kept me going.*

While at my mom's I continued to work on my transfers. Getting into my bed alone was impossible with the sliding board I was using, because of its weight combined with my lack of hand function, so I had a smaller one made. I had a handle added on it to assist in holding it. In no time, I was transferring on my own. It was hard but I was doing it.

Dropping anything was frustrating because my I could not bend over yet without falling out of my chair, and using a reacher was a tedious process. I remember the feelings of anger I felt when I dropped something. So to ease my frustration I would say thank you Father while picking something up and usually ended up with a smile on my face.

I was determined to get some independence back, which made Mom and my aides scared and angry at times. Mom was trying to make up for her absence from my life as a child and wanted to do everything for me, and thus we were in a constant power struggle.

People did not realize they were hindering me by wanting to help so badly. I knew I needed to keep trying and continue to stand up for myself. If I didn't use it I would lose it. Retraining my muscles and nerve pathways was my goal, and to do that I had to continue trying to do all that I did before.

I learned the hard way that when I rush I have close calls and sometimes would fall. I did so much of it my mom bought me a shirt with "If you can read this please put me back in my chair".

After my PT and OT goals were met, my therapy was discontinued. It was up to me to build on what I had learned. I religiously did my hand exercises three times per day and was constantly picking up different size beads and placing them in a soda bottle. That bottle of beads. I was determined to get my independence back.

Chapter 10. *Going It Alone*

After they carried me out of my house and in to my mom's my focus was on me and my continued physical healing.

I was in no shape to initiate ending my marriage, I was just glad to be out.

However I did recall all the threats and promises he made if I ever left. I watched how he handled his last divorce and he knew what he legally could do to punish her and his kids without being put in jail. I was always warned not to ever cross him and was afraid what would happen if I did.

My mom and I talked about initiating a divorce. I didn't care - I told her to do whatever she thought she should do. I wanted nothing to do with it.

My mom contacted her lawyer who initiated my divorce. It probably was a mistake not to be involved, but I just wanted to move on, focusing on my recovery.

After only being at Mom's for a few weeks, and having OT and PT every other day, suddenly all my therapy came to an abrupt stop. Keep in mind that at this time I still wasn't able to hold the phone up to my ear and keep myself from tumbling over at the same time.

I spent days on the phone with the lawyer and insurance company trying to straighten this all out. After several calls and a lot of frustration I discovered what he had done. He switched insurance companies and gave an inaccurate birthdate, so when they submitted for payment for my therapy it was immediately rejected.

He was still trying to control what was happening to me even though I was no longer under his roof.

Late at night after Mom was asleep my mom's phone would ring and I would hear his voice on the answering machine saying nasty things and wishing me harm. At this time in my recovery I was still not able to transfer in and out of bed alone, so I was forced to just lie there and listen to all that was said.

For some reason I was not able to cry when it was all happening, but today as I read this I have feelings that come to surface and I know I need to let it out.

Healing never seems to come until I say these things out loud. Before I went to Western PA I had to go to court one time. I was scared while my mom and my aide pushed me into the Gettysburg courthouse. Three policemen were close by my side ready to protect me if they saw the need. After we were inside, my eyes met his and all the fear came rushing back. The purpose of that day was to initiate the divorce. It is my guess that legally the judge needed to hear directly from me.

That meeting didn't last long, and that was the last time I would see him. Mom, my aide, and I left, never to return.

While he was at work, I asked my aide to get some things from the house I had left. Gary thwarted that from happening by staying home from work. He was there monitoring everything that she did. She left with nothing that day. He was going to have the last say.

He was going to decide what I could take and what would stay and to ensure that, he changed the locks that same day. Somehow Mom arranged for him to move some of my things onto the back deck where my mom and some of her friends could load them up and bring them back.

Things that were near and dear to my heart he would not let me have. My early family pictures, quilts, and clothing, along with precious family heirlooms were never given back. He thought he could use them as leverage to manipulate and control me. Although my mom wanted me to fight, I just walked away. I was glad to be out of that house.

I knew he was trying to make things so difficult for me that I would give up and beg him to take me back. He used a wife of his high school friend to visit me and she tried to talk me into going back.

While I was at UPJ, I was not forced to be at the courthouse for divorce proceedings, but instead was allowed to testify over the phone. This all took place between my classes.

I was still afraid, and shook as I made the calls.

Those calls initiated feelings I didn't want to deal with, so I pushed them all away. I immediately focused on my classes and physical therapy.

This craziness went on for too many years, and looking back now it is so clear to me how he used the teachings of the bible to manipulate and control me. Somehow I got through it, and I continue to hold on and find the part of me he couldn't smother. This was my time to thrive, and nothing he did was going to prevent me from living a life God wants me to live.

> *This was my time to thrive, and nothing he did was going to prevent me from living a life God wants me to live.*

It took a long time, but slowly I began to see why I was attracted to him and him to me. I see where I went wrong, and take responsibility for my fault.

I have come to terms with where I went wrong.

The way he treated me was just as wrong, but even still I wish him no harm.

"Start by doing what's necessary; then do what's possible, and suddenly you are doing the impossible."-- St. Francis of Assisi

Chapter 11. *Moving Again*

I was grateful to my mom for giving me a place to stay, but knew it was time for me to leave because I was drinking too much. Mom would close her restaurant and we would both begin drinking. Mom saw to it my glass stayed full of wine because I was not able to get it myself. My hands were still so weak I needed to use an adaptive cup with a handle on it that allowed me to slip my whole hand through. We didn't stop until usually one of us passed out.

One night we went to "sleep" and a few hours later awoke to the sound of my mother vomiting. I felt helpless, and days went by before I confronted her about my concern for our drinking. She agreed she had a problem also but made no plan to correct it. My drinking was consuming too much of my time so I decided to stop drinking and focus on my recovery.

I obsessively watched Joyce Meyer and returned to researching who I was in Christ. After spending a few months with my mom, I had to leave because the environment was still not conducive to healing. It had been a year since my SCI, and I wanted more, so I asked for assistance from the Center for Independent Living, and attended my first meeting. They gave me a contact at the Office of Vocational Rehabilitation, and they referred me to a technical institute for individuals with disabilities called the Hiram G Andrews Center, located in Johnstown, PA.

I had a nurse aide Jill, who became a good friend while she was helping take care of me at my mom's. She drove my mom and me in her spare time to Western PA to HGA. It was a cold, blustery January day with no snow on the ground at home, but as we got closer the snow was visible on the ground. The wind was blowing so hard it affected my balance while transferring out of the car. Jill had to push me into the building because I was not strong enough at that point to push myself, especially into that wind.

I met with my evaluator and completed the battery of tests. I was honest with her while expressing my concern that I didn't belong there. I saw a lot of children who had only mental and or emotional disabilities and only a few in wheelchairs with CP and MS. But there was no one with an SCI. They seemed so much worse off than I was. She convinced me to stay by offering me full time PT and OT. That was an offer I could not turn down.

The paperwork was complete and the plan all laid out. I made an agreement to return and stay for at least three months. We traveled back home and in a few months I would leave once more, but this time for good. The day finally came and it was time to say my goodbyes.

Jill and her husband packed my things in the car. I didn't own much because I had left a lot behind when I left my husband and my house. I said goodbye to my mom while she cried. I think she was more frightened than me and wanted me to stay and keep her company. For my own survival I had to leave regardless of how scared she was for me.

We pulled out of the driveway and I waved at my mom as we drove away. Leaving her was hard but it was the right thing to do. I had to swallow my tears and continue moving on. I was filled with hope and anxiousness of things to come, and that made each moment of doubt and fear easier to overcome.

The next few months I grew so much, continued to challenge myself, and was learning how to be independent again. I still was researching God's word, and daily I would find a verse that seemed to speak to me, and I would write it down. This kept my focus on all that was good and helped me through each day.

Before long I was doing my own laundry, cooking, and making my own bed, to name a few. My OT Jane helped me find ways to start sewing, crocheting, and even cooking again. I attended outings that included bowling and even adaptive jet skiing. I was living life again.

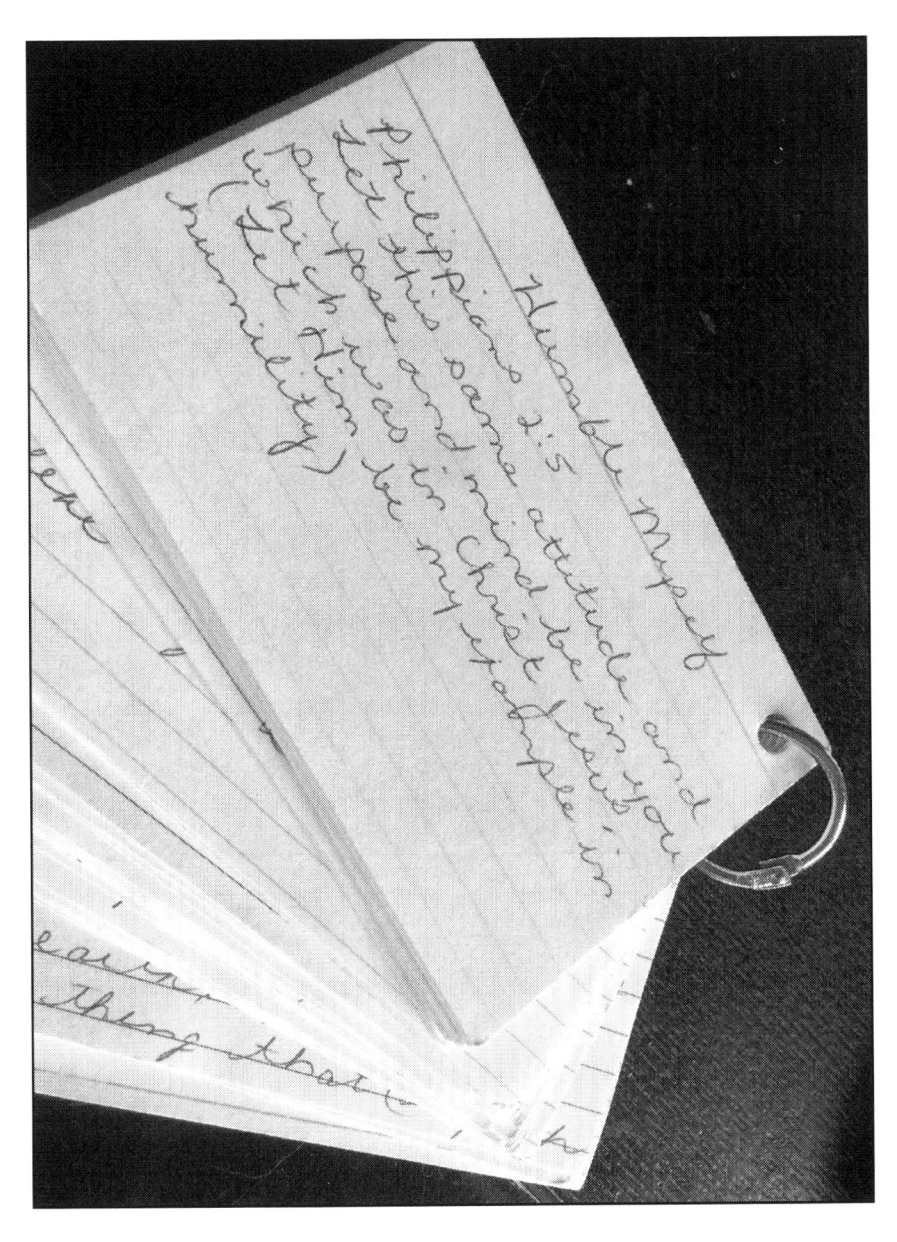

My Daily Verses

I was in a wonderful place and taking it all in. I learned how to use the public transportation system and started doing my own shopping. After a few months spring was here and I committed to learn how to drive again. For the next few months I attended driving classes which certified me to drive with special equipment.

Each step along the way was so exhilarating! The time finally came when we had to justify my stay at the center and justify continuing my PT and OT. That was not a hard thing to do because my OT Jane had written down all my accomplishments.

Next, I had to commit to attending three classes at the local community college and would travel back and forth using the bus.

At times I felt like I was on top of the world and doing things I never would have dreamed of. I had moments of pure joy because if it weren't for my SCI this would not be happening!

My sociology professor noticed my potential and urged me to apply at the University of Pittsburg in Johnstown. That was right across the street. I followed her lead and within a few months I was attending full time classes, and in between I attended OT and PT for as long as I could.

My schedule was so full I had no time feel sorry for myself. I was living on campus with the kids who partied on the weekends, but drinking was not an option for me. Thank goodness after I left my mom's the obsession to drink was removed.

Fear would crop up at times and when that happened I would force myself to just do whatever it was, even though afraid. I would repeat 2 Timothy 1:7 over and over. "God did not give me a spirit of fear and timidity but one of power, love and self-discipline" until my fear subsided.

I worked through every emotion like this. I had an index card for every feeling and the verse on it to dissipate that negative feeling. For example: for anxiety, I repeated Corinthians 7:32 "It is God's desire that I be free of all anxiety and distressing care."

This was the first step that helped me put my fears and anxiety in their proper place. I had to commit to stop living by how I felt or what I wanted and start living by God's word. I was careful with whom I associated. I continued to attended class, and in my spare time I was in PT and OT.

I had an aide who helped me get dressed in the morning before class and helped me to bed. I needed help with doors, taking notes, and basic tasks like turning lights off and on. I was still using my adaptive silverware, which was an embarrassment when eating in the cafeteria, so I was determined to learn how to eat without it. I awkwardly would hold a spoon, and did this for months until I regained the use of the muscles in my hand.

In this case, my pride helped me in the long run! I wanted more privacy, so I only had the aides come in the morning, decreasing my time to one visit per day. When I approached the director of the personal care agency I was using, she urged me not to decrease my hours, cautioning me that "once you give them up you will lose them." I didn't care, because I needed and longed to have my privacy back.

Against everyone's advice I decreased my hours, and was so glad I did. I reached a new level of gratitude and was enjoying my freedom. Listening to my gut was starting to pay off! (Before I move on I want to add that the director was wrong about my hours and I never lost them. An assessment is made, and if my needs increased or decreased the hours would change accordingly.)

I now believe that the personal care agency was not worried about me but instead their concern was losing billable hours from the state. The fewer hours I have, the less they get paid.

My goal was to function as a member of society. I lived on campus for two years, seldom returning home. I did not leave for spring break or holidays because of the drinking environment at my mom's. When I was at my mom's I had to be careful and I needed to guard against wanting or being offered that first drink.

Eventually I got lonely during the holidays, and decided to visit Mom. The only safe way for me to visit my mom was too have somewhere else to stay when I needed to get away from the booze. So I decided to visit my mom, but I would stay in a motel during my visit. I rented a handicapped accessible van and headed home, driving without a GPS. Still finding my home was an incredible achievement, and I was so proud of myself.

> *People can help support and guide me, but I am responsible to love and protect myself.*

I had a good visit with my mom and was never tempted to drink because I had somewhere to go when it was time for me to leave. Spending a week alone with no aides coming in and out was just what I needed and once again I was learning to trust myself and finding out how strong I was. People can help support and guide me, but I am responsible to love and protect myself.

All through my recovery I struggled with asking for help, and finally spoke to a dear friend who had over 35 years of sobriety. Toni asked me if it made me feel good to help someone. I said yes, of course. She continued, "Then don't deny others the right to feel good either." Thinking of it that way has made asking for help a lot easier and even today when I need help I remember that conversation and ask for what I need.

I realize that too much or too little of anything is not good for me, and try to seek balance in all things.

I have never been on a cathing schedule, because I still have bowel and bladder sensation, and this became a small issue at college. I did not have much time between classes, so when transferring off and on the toilet became too much I started using 16 inch catheters so I could just pull up in front of the toilet and cath directly from my chair. Getting my pants up and down was an issue in the winter, but in the summer life got a lot easier because I wore dresses.

Adjusting to life in a wheelchair and attending college at the same time was difficult, but I was doing it, and I was happy for the first time in a long time. I didn't visit my mom very much and even stayed on campus during Christmas and spring break. I enjoyed staying on campus along with the freedom it had to offer.

Also, going home meant I would miss PT and OT and my continued recovery was my priority. It was during this time that I experienced the freedom of swimming once again. Swimming was something I didn't think I'd ever do again until one day in physical therapy we got in the pool. I was expecting the worst, to sink as soon as I hit the water. To my surprise, I kept myself afloat and after a few minutes of realizing I had some control over my body movements, I turned onto my back and floated for few seconds.

Swimming Again!

My PT told me most SCI individuals cannot stay afloat. We were both surprised that my injury didn't compromise my ability to swim. I was elated that I could get from one point to another without being surrounded by metal. Slowly my fear and anxiousness was replaced with determination and much needed self-confidence in myself. After this experience, I started swimming on campus between classes every chance I got, and eventually completed 15 laps in an Olympic size pool.

Along with being excellent recreation therapy, swimming improves balance, coordination, provides muscle strengthening, and more importantly, it helps build self-confidence once again.

I had access to the bus here, but at home I was stuck in the house. I even needed help getting in and out of the house, so that was a deterrent to visiting home.

I found an AA contact and started attending meetings. Patti became my sponsor and eventually helped me start an AA meeting on campus that is still around today. Alcohol was not easily accessed on campus and with my classes and PT I had no time to even think about drinking. As a result I remained sober and celebrated four years of sobriety.

I had only one close call. I was on my way to buy a box of wine, and there was a lady on the bus who was visibly intoxicated. She was leaning to one side and had one eye closed to compensate for her double vision. Seeing her reminded me what it was like to be so intoxicated I could not see straight. The bus came to a stop where I was to get off and I just remained seated. Once again I had just witnessed the power of God working in my life.

Chapter 12. *Finding Tracy*

I decided it was time for me to move off campus and so I found an apartment located close to the college and moved with the help of friends who worked at the college. I continued attending AA on campus and eventually met my partner Tracy. We immediately formed a bond and have been together ever since.

Tracy and Me

I withdrew from college after my sophomore year was complete because I was unable to pass algebra even after hours of tutors. After taking the class four times I realized it was not within reach and used this as an excuse to drink. Eventually I told Tracy, and at my request she poured the alcohol down the sink.

This was an exciting time for me, having my own place. I started going to AA again and stopped drinking. In the meantime, getting home to see my mom was still an issue, and my mother would not drive here to visit me.

My brother did something I will forever be grateful for. He purchased a van and installed all the adaptive equipment for me and delivered it to me that summer. I still am overwhelmed with gratitude every time I get into my van because I remember what it was like waiting for the bus in the rain, cold, wind, and snow.

Life is good and I could not ask for more. A few months after that, Tracy and I decided to take our relationship to the next level, and I moved into her house across town. Our house is all one floor but there was a lot to do to make it all accessible to me.

Unfortunately, it wasn't long after that when I got devastating news that my mom suffered a stroke. Mom never pulled through and passed away within a few days.

I was grateful that she met Tracy before this all happened. I have faith that Mom knows I am just fine and is cheering me on from above. I used my inheritance to remodel our bathroom and kitchen making everything accessible. I still am so grateful to be able to pull directly up to a sink. I know Mom is smiling down on me today saying "You, my dear, inspire me" and "Have I told you lately you are one stubborn woman?"

Around this same time I was still grieving from losing my mom and I started to use my muscle relaxer to sleep. I made a decision to stop it and am not currently on any medication. I no longer take any medication of any kind. Muscle spasms are not an issue and I am blessed that I have minimal pain other than occasional shoulder pain from overuse.

Meeting Tracy has been a true blessing. Having her in my life has made me even more grateful for what I have than ever before. Fun is more fun when you have someone to share it with.

For example, over the recent Memorial Day weekend we got to spend some time at the beach. I welcomed the time to relax, to soak up some sun, and to reflect on how thankful I am for everything I have. It also encourages me to look forward to more progress, if that is in the plan!

Loving the Beach

Chapter 13. *AA Power*

When the thought of drinking crosses my mind I go back to basics and remember that to be an alcoholic I do not have to drink every day. For me, it's not how much or how often I drank. It's what it does to me when I do. Just the fact that I question my drinking is an indication of a problem. My alcoholism is like having cancer. If left untreated it gets worse, not better. The good news is I can stop my suffering by not taking that first drink.

It's important for me to remember how cunning, baffling, and powerful this disease is, and left to my own devices I will eventually get drunk. Thanks to AA and the people in it I have been given a second chance, and make a daily effort to see a blessing in everything. Recovering from my SCI and my alcoholism has been a blessing.

Through the twelve steps and all the amazing people in AA I have learned life is a constant process of uncovering, discovering, and discarding. The first time I was introduced to AA I really had an issue with God so I was told to use the group as my higher power, and I could do that. They were a power greater than me and definitely demonstrated all the things I longed to be.

After a while it was impossible for me not to believe in a power greater than me. God was working in my life and theirs, and realizing this I was no longer scared. Whenever I have my doubts they are wiped away after spending some time with others who are just like me. Hearing the stories and witnessing all the changes made it impossible for me to continue to deny the existence of God. I first came to realize, and then came to understand, how alcohol cuts me off from others and God. I saw and heard how He had changed other people in my group and eventually I saw the little ways He was working in mine. But for this to happen, I have to stay off the booze.

Today I worry about today, tomorrow I will worry about tomorrow, and never do I worry about yesterday! Lou Ann Grey told that to me one day when my anxieties were getting the best of me. I was blessed to have so much support and know without all of them and their support I would have thrown in the towel. I am grateful for AA and the individuals in it. They gave me the gift of living in today.

Sometimes if I am having a bad day I need to focus on living one hour at a time, some days one minute at a time. Today nothing is as overwhelming to me if I break it down. Drinking stunted my emotional growth because at age 39 I was functioning and living like I did in my youth. My problems were real and way too much to bear. I still did not know how to solve a problem, so I over reacted to everything and functioned accordingly.

First, I had to identify the problem, then find possible solutions and then identify the steps to effectuate the solution. In college, I relied on a smart pen to tape lectures and take notes. One day it broke and I had a mini crisis over it. A friend said to me, "Your smart pen not working is not a crisis. Your mother getting pancreatic cancer is." She helped me put things into proper perspective. For that I am grateful.

Chapter 14. *Paddling and Standing*

Tracy and I have experienced so much, and live each day to the fullest. We have gone white water rafting, been to the beach, and last year went kayaking for the first time. It was exhilarating maneuvering on the lake without being dependent on my chair.

Kayaking – No Chair!

It was around this time I decided to find a walker without my doctor's support, help, and advice. I just knew if I could push myself up, nothing but good could come from it. My goal was to get my muscles firing again and let my body take it from there. For over a month I called the local goodwill and visited the missions looking for a used walker. Finally I found one and after bringing it home decided it was not safe to use. My search continued.

I was talking with a friend sharing my recent findings, and my search for the perfect walker. Unknown to me she had a perfect new one that was ordered for her sick husband, and since he could not use it, she offered it to me. My search came to an end, and this was the beginning of continued healing for me!

Once I had the walker in my possession, I toyed with the idea of standing on my own by using the patio furniture to brace myself. I attempted to follow through with my plan until I lost my balance and almost fell. I had to get all my rushing emotions under control and save all my determination and strength to try this again when I had Tracy's assistance. That weekend my goal was met!

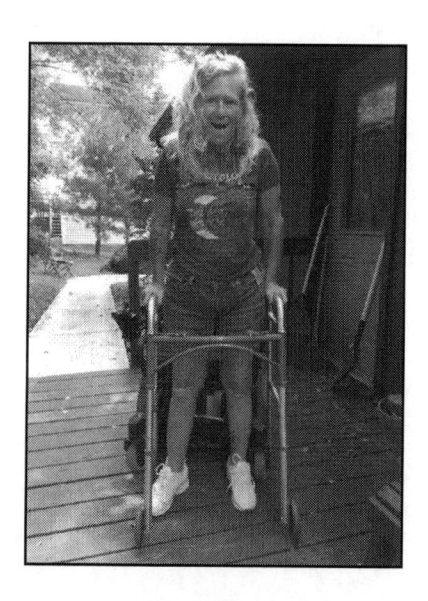

Me, Standing Tall

Over the years I have had found that there is always a way to do something; I must be creative enough to figure one out. I still use dycem pads to open things or just to get a better grip on something. I still use it to pull my leggings up over my waist. It's in every room of my house and on my person, always.

No longer do I take little things for granted, and still, after all this time, it doesn't take much to make me happy. When unloading the dishwasher or washing machine I say thank you after picking each item up and while putting it away, even if I don't feel like it. It always makes a mundane job easier and I usually end up smiling after I am half way through. Maybe I am different, but it took me losing everything to appreciate what a blessing it is to be able to perform basic tasks that most people consider simple and unrewarding.

I have learned a lesson in humility and accept where God puts me. I am always given the strength I need to get though any situation and am OK spiritually and emotionally no matter what's happening around me. Today I know and believe I have all the strength I will ever need and love how it is multiplied every time I share it!

Chapter 15. *I Am Stronger than My Struggles*

Life can seem easier at times when I'm not making as many waves and just settle for mediocracy. For instance, I've been seeing a doctor and knew it was time for a second opinion.

So I forced myself to step outside of my comfort zone and took a chance making that appointment. I left that appointment with a script for PT and OT and would soon be walking with my braces. I was close to canceling that appointment out of a lot of "what if's" and fear of the unknown. Long story short, my decision to go was a good idea and the right thing to do. She recommended an outpatient rehab that specializes in spinal cord injury and will focus and help me accomplish my goals.

When it's all said and done I have found that everything worked out. I left that appointment overwhelmed with tears. Not because I was sad but because I was grateful to God for giving me the strength to push on and do it in spite of my fears. God is always molding me into the person he wants me to be so my task is aligning my will with what He wants me to be. If he wants me to walk, I will walk, and if he doesn't, I won't. It's that simple and I'm OK with whatever He decides. Every day there's opportunity to grow and it's not always by leaps and bounds; usually it's in taking baby steps that lead to the pathway to freedom. It always starts with paying attention to the God consciousness within and doing the next right thing even when I don't feel like it.

I no longer accept the status quo in my recovery from my spinal cord injury and in my recovery from alcoholism. I dream big and I expect a lot from God and myself. If I would have listened to my doctor the day he told me, "you will never..." I certainty would not be doing most of the things that I am doing today.

I finally found a God of my understanding who loves me just for being me. He has shown me a way to be OK no matter what's going on around me or what my circumstances may be. He has taken my obsession to drink away and when I seek to do his will and not mine, anything is possible. It took me some time, but I have finally realized His will is always better than anything I could dream up.

The task is maintaining that reality, and I can only attain it if I stay away from the booze. If God wants me to take a few steps and eventually walk, I will. If God wants me to have a $12,000 chair to make my life easier, it will happen. I am OK where I am at, so if none of those things happen that's OK, too. It's a pretty amazing place to live and all I have to do to maintain that is not picking up a drink. Drinking shuts me off from experiencing God's Grace in my life. When I'm drinking, I am too sick and distracted to hear and listen to my own inner voice. God speaks to me there, and I know He cares. My life is a gift and is always good.

The blessings keep getting bigger since I have stopped my drinking. Once I start to drink I don't want to stop until I am completely numb, thus the viscous cycle continues. I drink, feel sick, and guilty, and then nothing gets done. I know for a fact that I would not be standing today if I were drinking. Drinking consumes too much time and sucks all the life out of me, allowing no room for anything else, and only causes me pain and suffering. I am grateful for my sponsor because I never had anyone to bounce things off of before, and never knew that's exactly what healthy people do. I am thankful she is always there to help me through. No longer do I second guess everything I do.

I've learned how to think things through and now am making rational decisions. I am so very grateful for all she has been willing to do.

Through this process of healing and self-discovery, I have experienced comfort in researching God's word. I was granted peace and lasting power because for the first time in my life I know who I am, and finally have a way to cope with whatever difficulty is thrown my way.

Today I work at staying grateful for the little things and no longer live by how I feel. I say "thank you Father" all day and every day, even when I don't feel like it. After saying thank you, I find my "feelings" catch up to my words and I do experience gratitude. So practice gratitude because it releases the neurotransmitter dopamine, which gives us that "Oh, do that again" feeling.

Journaling is valuable and paramount in maintaining my gratitude because any time I am feeling down, I read my journal and am reminded of how far I have come. Then I am left wanting more of the same.

I can tell you the first time I tied my shoe, buttoned my shirt, put on a pair of jeans, and zipped them up! Just recently I could hold and pour soda into my glass using my left hand; something I have not done since the day of my accident.

Keeping track of all my accomplishments and celebrating them feeds my gratitude and stops me from feeling sorry for myself. Today I no longer walk around feeling isolated and sick. One of the best things of all is that big ache is gone. I am no longer overcome by indecision and self-doubt, and don't operate under the misconception that other people know more than me.

> *I am no longer overcome by indecision and self-doubt, and don't operate under the misconception that other people know more than me.*

God gave me the gift of that still voice inside, so I listen to that when I am unsure. Others have answers, but I have found they are not for me. This way of operating is sometimes foreign and strange until I refocus and let God be my guide. When I do this today my life is good, God never dumps too much in my path; well, at least not all at once.

Because I am not drinking I am able to see God working little miracles in my life and in those around me. The constant fog I lived in because of alcohol of has gone away. And each day I wake is a new day. I have always been granted all the love, protection, and care to get through.

More gratitude is always within reach when I take a step back and shake off my grief. Seeking God's will in all that I do allows me to live a perfectly fine life full of goodness. My peace of mind and serenity is tied directly to my level of acceptance of whatever is happening in my life. Life is hard no matter what one's circumstances may be, and a lot easier when I accept that this is the way things are supposed to be. When I do that, I am granted all that I need, and have an abundance of comfort, peace, and power, even for another person who may have a need.

Chapter 16. *My New Normal*

What I once believed were unattainable gifts and only available to only a chosen few have been given to me through a new way to move. Thinking things through was not something I was taught to do. I must creep before I crawl, and crawl before I can learn how to stand tall.

My new way of life is a blessing in disguise. What others see as distraction and distress has been transformed into accomplishment and success. The people I have met are too innumerable to count, but no matter where life takes me, I will be forever bonded with a few. If reading that thought softens your heart and makes you smile you know who you are and I want to say thank you!

To strangers looking at my life from the outside in, it may appear my world has grown smaller but that is a misconception.

Going Rafting

My phone is filled with an equal number of doctors, rehabs, and friends. I choose to look at this as a resource and not a negative consequence.

Today I have all the help a girl could ask for available to me. And for that I am grateful.

Because of my spinal cord injury, I have experienced white water rafting, kayaking, and jet skiing to name a few. I continue to hike the local trails in my sports chair, swim, garden, and practice yoga. These are all tasks I did before my accident and still do today; the only difference is I am doing it from a wheelchair. Nevertheless, I'm doing it!

Accomplishing simple tasks requires planning and forethought, and as a result I've been forced to form new habits and ways of operating which make me live more simply. My SCI has required me to become mindful of each and every action I take, and for that I'm grateful. When I move I do it on purpose, and so I am constantly evaluating if it's worth the effort and time.

> *Once I started taking care of myself I noticed I continued to heal.*

A few years ago I stopped having aides in and out of my house for a few reasons. First, I came to the realization they were hindering me instead of helping me. They were quicker accomplishing certain tasks but I soon realized quicker doesn't mean better for me. Once I started taking care of myself I noticed I continued to heal.

Last year I learned to put on jeans and zipper them up. The zipper was difficult to hold on to, so I used dycem to pull it up. Today I can say I no longer need that aid. Practice truly does make perfect! It may take me a minute to button my shirt but the more I do it the better I get at it. So again, quicker is not better!

I have turned the most basic tasks into spiritual processes and experiences. The task of opening a can involves dicem for a better grip, my chin to stabilize it, and a table low enough that I could lean on. With every turn I say Thank You. For small cans it takes seven Thank You's and for larger ones it can take up to 16 Thank You's! Laundry involves saying anywhere up to 50 Thank You's because I get each piece out one at a time with my reacher.

Depending on my time, I will use my weaker hand to move the laundry, and this only intensifies my sense of gratitude because it requires me to demand more of my body and use my fine motor skills. The more difficult something is the greater the reward when I do it. I'm grateful for my SCI because without it I would not be living a life I am. Today I enjoy being me and I'm happy to say that I am finally free. Celebrating my life has been the key to my freedom. We all have those keys if we only take the time to stop and listen.

Chapter 17. *Alternative Healing*

In 2011, I suffered a small full thickness tear in my distal supraspinatus tendon, a tear in my subscapularis tendon, and a tear in the superior labrum in my right shoulder. I was living on campus and used my manual chair for exercise when I was not in classes. I was determined to wheel up a hill without help and the result was the three tears.

The pain was excruciating. I could not raise my arm, and needed help with basic tasks once again. I started OT and when that did not help my doc wanted to send me to a surgeon, claiming that was my only option.

He had no idea what he was asking me to commit to. Without the use of my arms I would be completely immobile for at least a year. My arms are like my legs now, and I cannot function without them. I had spent the last four years regaining my independence and could not even imagine a year of self-imposed helplessness.

I fervently searched for another answer online. After sharing my dilemma with my sociology professor, she referred me to her life coach. She reaffirmed that an operation was not necessary and stressed our body's amazing healing qualities. I had faith, and from that day on expected my body would heal in its own time, thus defying doctor's recommendations and not scheduling surgery.

Per her advice I bought therapeutic oil and massaged my shoulder daily along with faithfully doing my strengthening exercises given to me by my OT. Before she discharged me, I purchased a TENS unit and used that daily also. After eight months, my shoulder had healed.

I still have flare-ups when I ask too much of my body at the gym or on the track. I have accepted the occasional discomfort and am willing to tolerate it until the ice and naproxen does its job. Other than shoulder pain, I have no pain except for the normal aches and pains that go along with ageing. For that I am grateful.

Chapter 18. *Cultivating Gratitude*

When I slip into self-pity or just a depressive state I try to focus on what is good in my life and not my feelings.

I remind myself I am not alone and that everyone is dealing with a disability, no matter if it's visible or not. The only thing different about me is that mine you can see. All of us struggle in some shape or form and have found ways to overcome our adversities.

I'll look around me and if I see that one of my friends or family has a need, I try and fill it. Sometimes it's just listening, a phone call, smile, or a hug to let them know they're not alone. I have found when I do this it helps me also.

I've kept journals and logs of things that I've accomplished over the weeks, months, and years. I'll glance through them and reflect on how far I've come, and my gratitude is always renewed. No matter what I am going through, I look until I find something to be grateful for.

> *No matter what I am going through, I look until I find something to be grateful for..*

There's always something good about my day even if it's the most minute thing. It could be something as simple as giving thanks for being able to run my fingers through my hair and style it myself. It still doesn't seem like it was that long ago that that was an impossible task I thought I'd never accomplish. When I focus on all my blessings and not my burdens it keeps me humble and free of burdens.

> *"The very least you can do in your life is figure out what you hope for and the most you can do is live inside that hope. Not admire it from a distance, but live right in it, under its roof."* Barbara Kingslover

Determination and perseverance has paid off, because today I am completely independent and can do everything I did before my accident; just a lot slower. I practice adaptive yoga to help with range of motion and a way to connect with my body by simply noticing. It has accelerated my physical and emotional healing.

No longer do I need a drink or a drug to numb my feelings and alter my mood. Denying my feelings is dangerous; doing that will eventually cause me to pick up a drink.

I am living my life without aides coming in and out. I cook, clean, and take care of my house. I am also thankful for being able to drive again with hand controls. I have found the more I use my arms and hands the more functionality I get back.

After 10 1/2 years my doctor finally agreed that I may benefit from KAFO (Knee, Ankle, Foot Orthosis) braces. It was an emotional experience, because I did not see braces in my future because of the lack of support from my physiatrist. When I shared with him about getting some feeling back in the bottom of my feet his response was, "You can be a patient the rest of your life, or just get on with it." I didn't react to his comment but it made me angry and fueled me to prove him wrong.

> *My chair may sometimes break down, but I do not!*

Setting goals and accomplishing them is my life now, and I can either accept that and move on or be angry, miserable, and stagnant. Today I choose to stay positive. My truth today involves healing and to maintain that I will continue to set my goals and pursue them. God brought me this far and it's up to Him to decide how much I heal.

Through the 12 steps of AA I have identified what steals peace, and each morning when I wake, my task is to seek peace and pursue it with the same determination I had when drinking. My melt-downs today last a few minutes, while before they could go on for days, weeks, or even months. My chair may sometimes break down but I do not! No longer do I let my circumstances dictate my feelings and, as a result, I am in control of myself and my life, and am able to experience an amazing life by remaining grateful no matter where God puts me. As long as I stay sober I will continue sharing my experience, strength and hope.

Chapter 19. Accept, Adjust, and Move On, or Fight, Resist, and be Discouraged

As individuals, we are each unique and were given special gifts that were meant to be shared. We are tasked with discovering, uncovering, and discarding anything that is not God's will for us. Embracing that uniqueness and using it to improve society and others is my goal.

When I share my gifts, I am blessed every time because my own spiritual growth is accelerated and I am left with the feeling of wanting more. God gave me free will and it's up to me how I choose to use that will. Today I know God's will for my life is to help restore hope and gratitude to every person God brings into my life. Today humility is something I seek to attain and is something I desire, instead of recoiling from it. I've learned to accept right where God puts me and am OK no matter what is going on around me. This is a peace that can only come from God.

> *Today I know God's will for my life is to help restore hope and gratitude to every person God brings into my life.*

I've gone from being the victim to the victor and know that I am free and have the power to start my day over when things are not going well. For that I am grateful.

For six months I was using my AFO braces and a walker to stand only a minute at a time, and only by utilizing my upper body strength. My knees would bend when I distributed weight through my legs, and if I didn't hold myself up I would collapse on the floor.

Then later I was fitted for a type of brace called KAFO. These braces kept my knees locked which in turn let me distribute more weight through the legs. Regardless, when I did rise to my feet, the feeling I experienced was exhilarating and always renewed my hope, if only for that minute and a half.

I have had to get creative to accomplish that and I know the doctor would never approve because of what I had to do. I needed to be six inches higher to stand from my chair so I would transfer onto my bed then add a yoga mat and an extra cushion onto the one that is already on my chair. Then I would transfer back onto the chair and then was at a more comfortable height to stand. I placed the walker up against the bed to be more secure and then could push myself up. It's the best feeling in the world when I stand upright, so I will continue to push myself. There is no feeling on earth more fulfilling than that. After this experience I just knew it was time to search for a new doctor.

So I had to practice what I've learned, take a chance, and do something I was afraid to do. Thanks to the Internet and a few new friends I found a physiatrist specializing in the treatment of spinal cord injury. The downfall is that it meant traveling an hour and a half away. Because of my unfamiliarity with Western PA, I was anxious, but knew this was meant to be. I drove in silence while dreaming of what's ahead. It was a relaxing drive and just a beautiful February day reaching 58 degrees.

I went to that appointment in spite of my fear, and left with several scripts. One was for PT for gait training to learn how to walk again, and one for OT to build my arm strength which will guard against re-injuring my shoulders. It is standard procedure to have a bone density test after the ten-year mark, so that was in my future. She answered all my questions and when I left I finally had some direction. I could not have asked for more.

Leaving that office, I was experiencing a combination of exhilaration, gratitude, hope, and relief. I made my way to the entrance and waited for the valet to bring my van to me. A few tears trickled down my cheek because I was so close to accepting other people's mediocracy and "good enough." If I had given in to my fear and doubt I would have missed out. For that I am grateful.

Living life with a spinal cord injury can be like being caught up in a whirlwind. My SCI has created in me what seems to be an insatiable appetite for more freedom and longing to gain my independence. From experience, I know miracles can happen when I use my will correctly.

Never will I forget my first time on the beach sitting by the shoreline, listening to the waves break. I still cherish the rush of positive emotions I experienced while sitting up high on that adaptive beach wheelchair. I am grateful for my experience, but now I long to sit in the sand without being four feet above the beach and surrounded by plastic.

Tracy and Me on the Beach

I expected and welcomed all those feelings from my first time to come rushing back, and I knew along with it I would have a desire for more. I am looking forward to finding a way to sit in the sand and experience once again what it feels like to have grains of sand falling between my toes and fingers! For that I am grateful!

For the next six months I spent a lot of time trying to schedule an appointment with a company called ReWalk. They developed an exoskeleton suit that the patient can wear that will facilitate walking. Eventually an appointment was scheduled and I passed the evaluation, so my new appointment time was then set. This was just too good to be true!

Chapter 20. *The Reason*

Even though we don't see it, everything happens for a reason. All I am asked to do is continue through the seasons. Keep trudging ahead and always forging forward is so very important.

Today I found out I have what it takes to stand tall. In a few days, I will be walking with the help of a soft exoskeleton suit. After all this time, I still can recall the freedom I felt before my fall.

I miss the feel of Mother Earth beneath my feet and I am counting the days until I take my first steps. The excitement won't come to an end any time soon because next Tuesday before noon I will be picking up my KAFO braces. My blessings are many and I continue to bloom. Now I know we are never too old for blessings to unfold.

Finally I See

I am looking forward to accomplishing something new. There are many blessings sprouting up all around. While my past is full of them, I frown when I say, "How I wish I would have written them all down."

Now able to look back, I can see how God always had my back. He is always working in my life even when I was doing way too much worrying.

With each blessing I receive, I can see how each one has renewed me.

Slowly I know I am being called home with each step I take. I pray for endurance and wait in a state of amazement with each passing day.

All that matters now is what I do today and writing things down has become my new way. The days are few when I feel like all is lost but now I will have a way to restart. I am so glad I persisted even when I felt like resisting.

I am still amazed when I discover a new gift. It fills me up and carries me through, making me feel a feeling I never knew. It can't be packaged or bottled up, and it can only be shared when given away. Life is not hard when I listen to my heart and do what it wants. My job is to block out the noise and focus on my joys. Life is too short to fret and stumble, so open your eyes and accept the prize. For after all, life is a free gift always available to all.

I have four days to go until I stand tall, no matter what happens, I will be OK, and just knowing that always keeps me safe from harm.

Before You Start Your Day

Just wanted to say good morning, I hope you have a wonderful day!

We need to enjoy the sun while it shines, so that it can carry us through the tougher times! I woke up early and found I have a new gift that lifts me up when I am feeling down. I've always loved writing but needed reminding that the power in words are always transforming. One step at a time is all I need to continue growing and always moving forward.

...if you want to survive you must reach to thrive.

Feeling alone and apart from God is not normal, so push it aside and choose the divine. Always search for things that lift you up and feed your soul. What keeps us young is our sense of wonder. Cherish and be exactly who God wants you to be and don't be afraid to step out into the sun. God is always there and waiting for you to come.

Sometimes we must risk looking silly so that we continue growing. Standing still and staring for too long is so often unfulfilling. Keep your head up and looking forward, knowing if you want to survive you must reach to thrive.

God's will is not filled with confusion, so the right direction is now easier to find. Listening to my soul is now my ultimate goal.

Chapter 21. *Walking at Last!*

Time passed so very slowly while waiting for my opportunity to walk in the XO skeleton suit.

I had a twinge of fear of injuring my arms and was praying that my big day would soon be here. Up until that time I had to be careful how I moved and I limited the tasks that I performed around the house. Doing the laundry or the similar chores I would not do for fear of injuring my shoulder and arms.

I read my PT's instructions so that I was prepared to give it my all when I finally stand tall.

I was filled with awe every time I thought of standing tall. My tears would begin to flow and I'm still grateful beyond words for having had that experience. My emotions were strong and I knew it was not wrong. I've learned it's OK to feel and just let it go; it's one of the most beautiful feelings I have ever known.

What a beautiful life God has asked me to live; so much support surrounded by all that is good. Family and friends are cheering me on, all of them constantly wishing me nothing but the best. I'm happy to share this miracle that's called life and this miraculous moment to all those who care. I feel so much hope and gratitude in my heart. My journey has been so long but I knew all along because of my commitment that eventually this day would come.

I couldn't wait to stand without a walker in my chair and will forever cherish my time only be surrounded by air.

I had a bit of anxiety on how it would go. I did know my job was to be fully present in the moment and take it all in. I wanted to feel every emotion that came over me. Not just that special day but forevermore I will remain grateful and peaceful because after all is said and done the only thing in life we can control is how we feel and react when life unfolds.

Unfortunately, I got an early morning phone call from the gentleman at ReWalk. He had to cancel my appointment due to a family emergency. He was apologetic while saying this has never happened before. I was disappointed but know nothing happens by accident, so I was just fine.

I resolved to remain anxious and grateful all at the same time. I believe every day is a gift when we know and believe we are exactly where we should be. Even if you must pretend, that is OK, because eventually it will become your new reality. Not looking back, or even forward, but remain in the right here and now.

> *Today is a gift that's given to all, so make it your job to never fall.*

Yesterday is gone and tomorrow just a dream, so my job is to stay in today and make it all that it should be. Today is a gift that's given to all so make it your job to never fall.

Find out what you were called to do and give it your all, so that living each day of life benefits all.

Each day is a new day to start over new. I would walk someday soon but for a little while it was my job to sit back and just practice gratitude. They would contact me to let me know of my new date. Until that day came I kept my head up and worked on getting stronger. I was so thankful for all that I had been blessed to do!

Finally, the day came! I want to ReWalk and walked in the exoskeleton suit. My life once again took another turn in a positive direction after the experience of walking in the exoskeleton suit. It was wonderful to be up on my feet once again!

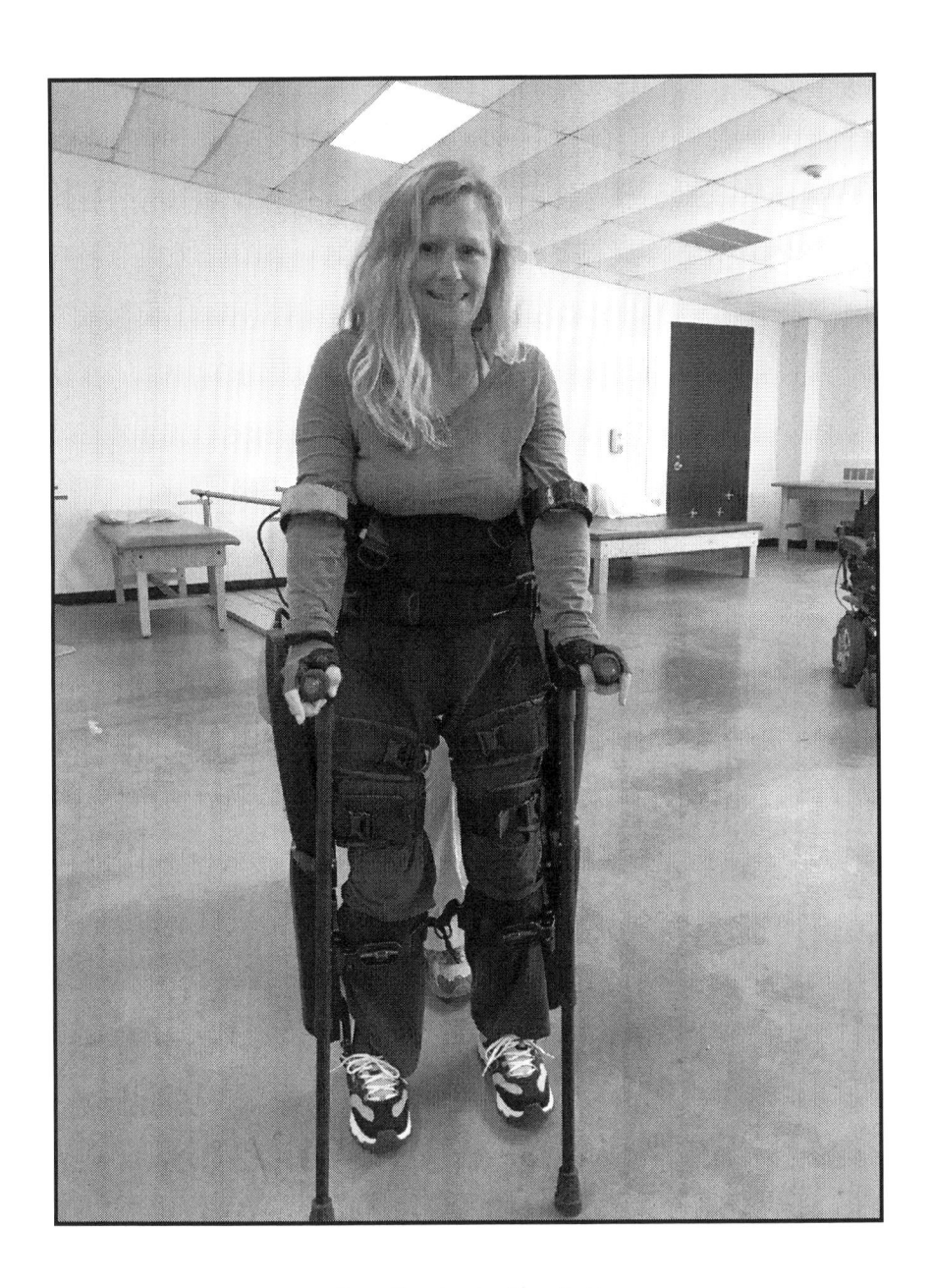

Standing in the Exo Suit

Chapter 22. *My Next Journey: Braces and a New Chair*

My braces were ordered and were delivered to me after only waiting a few short weeks. I must confess I did call twice a week to try and push the process along. I apologized for bugging them so much, but they seemed to understand. The receptionist said in a gentle tone that I would be the first to know when they finally arrived.

Patience is a gift that I've started perfecting. I've learned that everything that happens in God's time and not mine turns out better than I could have ever expected. Even on the day my appointment with ReWalk was postponed my day turned out to be productive regardless.

Because of my ReWalk contact at Harmerville, I was introduced to a new wheelchair company. He made the trip to visit me and assessed all my needs. I am looking forward to a new chair designed just for me. I'm especially looking forward to having a seat elevator. I am anxious to experience what it's like to possess the ability to raise myself up when need be and see and reach things because of that added mobility.

Early in my recovery I thought others knew what was best for me but since then I have found out differently. Advocating for myself has been a valuable lesson for me to learn. It's an important quality to have no matter who you are, but I have found it is necessity for those of us who are differently abled and have special needs.

I was finally notified that my KAFO (Knee, Ankle, Foot Orthosis) braces had arrived. I went to pick them up the very next day! Soon I stood with the help of my walker!

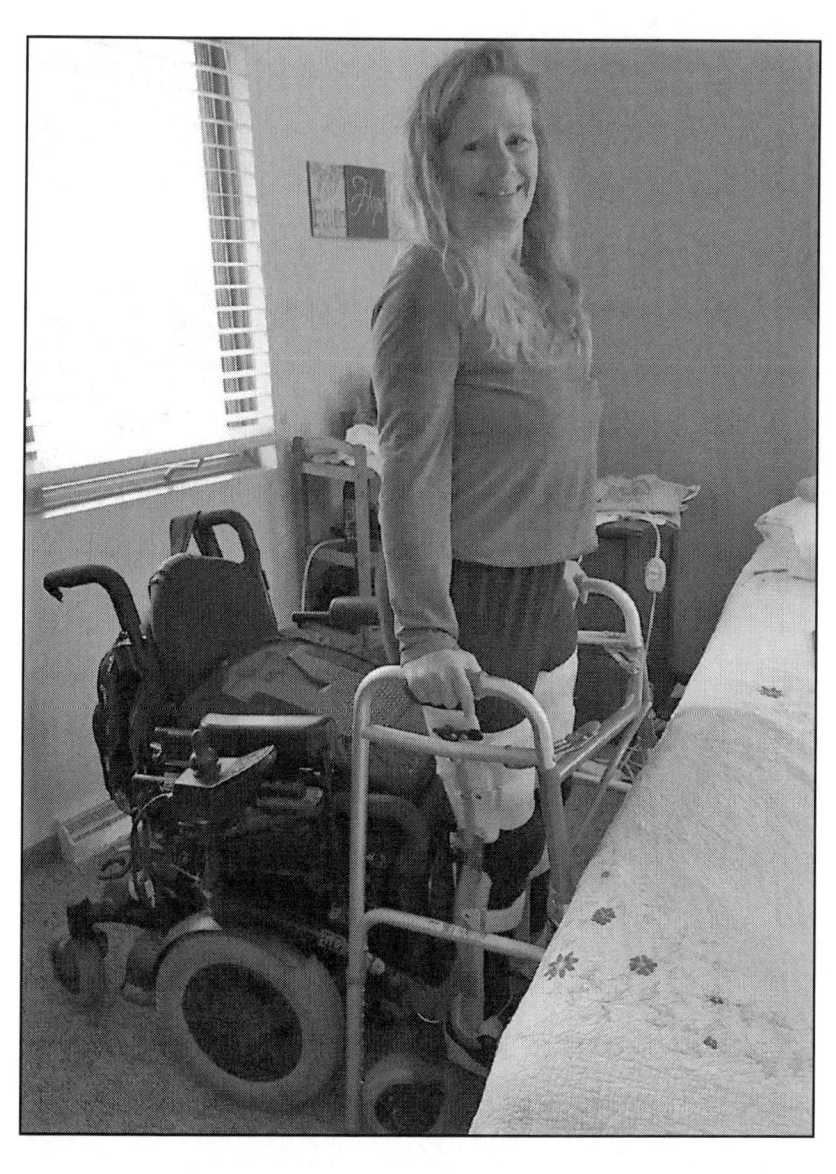

Standing with my KAFO Braces

Most of my book writing has been done right from the spot I'm standing in right now. Using my standing frame every day for an hour a day has helped me regain muscle mass, and has improved my abdomen control.

In My Standing Frame

So if you're newly injured and have access to one, use it all you can, because if we don't use it we will lose it. The more we use it and get those muscles firing the more we get back; it's a simple as that.

After standing for an hour, and for the first time ever, the muscles on the top of my left foot are twitching as long as I am thinking to myself to try and move my ankle up and down. I have been doing this imaging for years and occasionally had movement. Not much, but it's not how much or how little progress I make, it's all about progress no matter how slow.

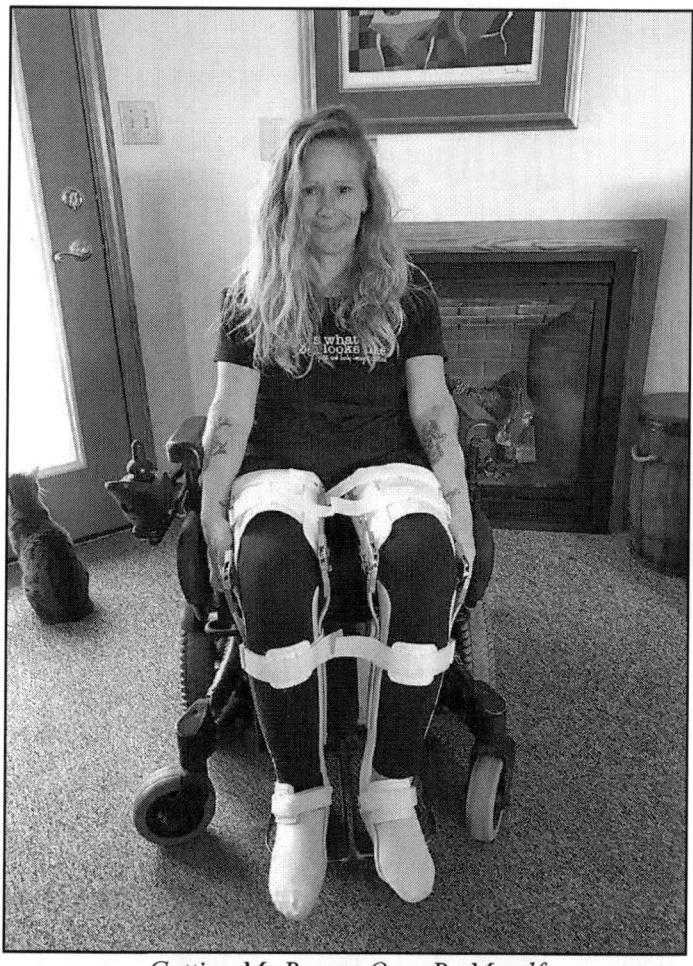

Getting My Braces On – By Myself

I was instructed not to stand on my own when alone, and instead practice putting my braces on and off. After doing this a few times it got easier and less cumbersome each time! Practice makes perfect!

Being Mindful

After one week of living life in my new chair with my elevating seat, standing directly from my chair made walking a much easier task to accomplish, and the result was setting new records while walking in PT. I walked a total of 96 feet with 24 feet being the longest stretch at one time. That was quite an accomplishment after sitting in a chair for 10 years!

Concurrently, I was participating in mindfulness training, and it couldn't have come at a better time. When the chair was delivered, I watched with fear and anxiety as the service guy took my old chair and security away, knowing that my life was going to get a lot tougher.

Everything was more difficult in my new chair, and it really slowed me down and forced me to be mindful of how I move and how quickly I do it. The consequence for not doing that would be falling on the floor. I've been there and done that and even have a T-shirt that says on the back of it, "if you can read this put my butt back in my chair" because the first year someone was always picking me up off the floor. It still makes me smile today.

I never thought I'd be dealing with troubling feelings once again. At times I felt like I did during the first year after my injury and was reliving a few of the same feelings and thoughts of how difficult everything was once again. My mindfulness training couldn't have come at a better time. I was reminded that thoughts are just thoughts and that my feelings can lie to me. That training has taught me to pay attention to my own thought patterns so I would not live in them and play them out over and over again. I was aware of the feelings but not identified by them.

The universe always gives me what I need when I need it. Shauna Shapiro talked about Mindfulness with the Attention to Intention to be curious, kind, and compassionate, even if my circumstance are not how I want them to be and even if I am not how I want myself to be, I can hold all of it with kindness and respond accordingly. I was right back to what I think about grows. I am either building good neural pathways or negative ones with every thought I think.

I needed to work on accepting my experience and my reactions even though I didn't like what I was feeling and going through at the time. After 10 years of being completely independent, these feelings caught me off guard. Regardless, I identified my wheelchair issues and trusted that in time they would be resolved and trusted that this too shall pass. I knew that when my thinking was right, all would fall into its proper place.

My focus was to be more curious, kind, and compassionate towards myself and my new wheelchair experience, while embracing and accepting each new struggle exactly as it was, just a few temporary challenges to resolve and overcome.

After 10 years I couldn't believe this was finally happening. As I was preparing to leave for my appointment and gathering my things to get out the door I thought to myself "I wish I would have invited someone to take along to capture this all on film. For a few seconds I wished I had someone close to me there to share in my happiness."

> *Studying videos of my progress has helped me figure out how to do some things better.*

Immediately following that thought was "I am not alone. I'm never alone and there will be a next time as soon as next week." In the meantime, I will find a friend who is willing to go along and take a few pictures and video. Studying videos of my progress has helped me figure out how to do some things better.

I still smile when I think of what I accomplished, and I'm feeling very happy. My physical therapist asked me why didn't I do this 10 years ago, why now? I attributed it to my doctor. He has his reasons and disbelief.

I always knew deep down that this was possible for me, and refused to ruin that happy moment with could have, should have, would have.

Every day is a new day, and I must stay away from blaming, because I cannot afford that negative internal dialogue. It's not conducive to creating and maintaining a healing environment. I am grateful for each and every one of the 23 steps I have taken.

Halfway through my walking, I was overcome with emotion and my physical therapist said "Please don't cry. I won't know what to do." I held back my tears and continued taking a few more steps no matter how hard I had to struggle. I asked my physical therapist Kelly if she was OK. She was working just as hard as me holding onto the gate belt around my trunk while offering me support and keeping me upright. I could not have done it without her assistance. I moved my legs and held myself up and know in time I will get stronger and no longer need help stabilizing my trunk. I then started occupational therapy and would then do exercises to strengthen my trunk and arms, so eventually I could walk unassisted.

My emotions and exhilaration were running high, and I realized that I had to force myself to slow down because I have a tendency to rush and get things done. Even my PT asked me if I was always this way.

Not in the sense that I wanted to get it over with. I just want to do more and will push myself to the point where it can be unhealthful. It's just something I must watch out for, because if I don't discipline myself I will be disciplined by something or someone else.

Sometimes I wake and my muscles are sore, but I am still feeling very grateful and could not ask for more when I think of walking again, thinking about my experience. I was already planning what I needed to do next time to make things easier. I needed to push the walker instead of trying to pick it up, and slow down. To do that I started saying thank you with each step I take.

Through the years, saying "thank you" has helped me in so many ways, and I was sure it would help me slow down. When I have rushed things I messed up, so it's important for me to slow down, stay determined and strong, and continue to prove them all wrong!

Practicing Mindfulness

I was in my eighth and final week of my mindfulness training, and it was the perfect time to reflect on all that I had learned and to decide how I would continue to implement these tools into my daily living.

Being mindful or practicing mindfulness does not mean peacefulness or that I will be at peace. It means I am accepting the situation, myself, and others exactly the way they are, not the way I want them to be or wish them to be. It means to stop fighting with my emotions to let them ebb and flow over me and through me so that I can be transformed by them and not stuck in them.

> *When I do not know who I am, I serve you. When I know who I am, I am you.—Indian Proverb*

Meditation on a daily basis has made me more compassionate towards myself and therefore I have found I am more compassionate and kind to others. Whatever I may be facing throughout each day I've found that I'm not so quick to react and my emotions remain intact. What used to be a one to two minute meltdown has now become a few seconds. After one of the lessons, I was introduced to the STOP acronym, which means:

STOP

S: Take stock (what am I feeling?)

T: Take a breath and notice my breathing.

O: Open and observe. Expand my awareness outward. What's happening around me? What are the sounds I hear? What is positive?

P: Proceed/new possibilities. Continue without expectations while asking myself how are things right now?

In doing this I found that it takes me out of my thoughts and back into my senses. This has helped me, and is an aid when I am in physical therapy and walking. Sometimes my thoughts can take over and I'm thinking to myself this is hard, I am tired, my arms hurt, I don't know that I can do this, I got to sit down blah blah blah. So when I noticed that thought process starting, I immediately bring my attention to my senses. I focused on what does it feel like when I'm taking that first step? And my breathing? What sensations am I feeling in my legs as I bear weight through them and as my feet make contact with the floor? When I focus on the tingling in my feet and throughout my legs and stay away from the random thoughts I'm able to stand tall and walk longer distances.

I was so grateful that I was finally at peace and comfortable in my new wheelchair. Like everything, it has its advantages and disadvantages, and I can honestly say the pros outweigh the cons.

Most importantly, it was a wonderful aid in physical therapy and it enabled me to walk longer distances without a break.

Just a few weeks later, It's still amazes me what I accomplished next. Not only did I set a new walking record of 197 feet, I walked 48 feet without taking a break. Then I successfully navigated two right corners without any help from my PT!

To top it off, I also set a standing record of 9 minutes and 5 seconds after I did all that walking.

For reasons I cannot explain I know in my soul that on that day I turned another corner in my recovery. Walking was just different in a good and profound way. I was moving with a bit more ease and was slowly gaining in confidence.

After each and every step I took I was anxious to find out what was next!

After three months, my physical therapy would soon be coming to an end, which meant a new chapter in my life was going to begin.

> *When this process was complete the result was more peace, freedom, and more space for healthy and productive thoughts.*

I was excited to see what God had in store for me next. From past history I know when I seek and do God's will, whatever happens I will have all the strength I need to get through whatever difficulty may cross my path.

Nothing ever goes away until it teaches me what I need to learn. Physical Therapy had ended but there was still a lot of healing I needed to do. My 20-year-old thought patterns were in the way of my spiritual and emotional growth. I had to go deeper. It was now time to identify my top 10 "go to" thought patterns. One by one I identified and labeled them. For instance, when the thoughts of "I'm all alone, I always have been and always will be" thinking started I labeled it as my "sick little girl thinking." Once they had labels it was easy to stop the destructive thought patterns as soon as they started.

After completing this process, I was empowered once more by being reminded that thoughts are just thoughts; they are not truth. It's one thing to say that and another to identify and recognize that I'm having those thoughts. Until I completed that process I could not change. When this process was complete the result was more peace, freedom, and more space for healthy and productive thoughts.

Cherishing Each Step: A Chronology

"Our deepest fear is not that we are inadequate. Our deepest fear is that we are powerful beyond measure. It is our light, not our darkness that most frightens us. We ask ourselves, "Who am I to be brilliant, gorgeous, talented, fabulous?" Actually, who are you not to be? You are a child of God. Your playing small does not serve the world. There is nothing enlightened about shrinking so that other people won't feel insecure around you. We are all meant to shine, as children do. We were born to make manifest the glory of God that is within us. It's not just in some of us; it's in everyone. And as we let our own light shine, we unconsciously

give other people permission to do the same. As we are liberated from our own fear, our presence automatically liberates others." – Marianne Williamson

I found out that for the next two months I would be traveling four days a week to PT and OT, spending two hours a day driving there and back.

All of my healing has happened in God's time and not mine. I have found life is so much more enjoyable when I slow down and practice being fully present in the moment. Remaining present and focusing on my senses and not my thoughts is the only way for me to master walking once again.

A few months ago I took my first steps and could only walk a total of 23 steps in increments six feet, then ten feet and lastly seven feet. A few weeks later I went a total of 119 feet with 36 feet being the longest stretch, and after another few weeks was up to nearly 200 feet! While I'm walking, my senses are heightened and with each step I take I experience strong tingling that starts in the balls of my feet, travels to my heels, and continues up my legs. I've noticed that when I am taking my last walk at PT my muscles are starting to get the idea of what to do and how they are supposed to respond.

At that moment, I can feel all of my muscles firing and working together the way God intended it to be. It feels wonderful and still amazes me!

Standing up and walking is getting a bit easier. I was told by my PT that she doesn't have to help very much anymore, and I am thankful I am now doing most the work.

My job for now is to focus on my breath and keeping my head up, because this aids in proper body alignment and makes moving forward a little easier. After each step, I pause while being mindful of what I am experiencing and take it all in. Moving one leg even a few inches at a time is still exhilarating!

> *After each step I pause while being mindful of what I am experiencing and take it all in.*

I never appreciated how amazing my body was until I have had to relearn how to move and walk again. Something that was once so automatic has now become an arduous task at times and can take me back to the early days of my recovery when moving my hands and fingers seemed to be an unsurmountable task.

I am teary eyed as I write. I am so very grateful for all my new healing! Never will I give up. And now I have somewhere to turn when I start feeling down! The twitching I am now experiencing is just the next phase of my healing since my injury, and for now I will sit back and wait and continue giving thanks. May God watch over and keep you safe from harm.

Getting sound answers on what direction to take or not to take always happens in God's timing, not mine. The answers only come when I slow down, and practice being fully present in the moment. Focusing on how I'm feeling as I'm walking is the only way for me to eliminate any lingering fears I may have. The fear of succeeding can sometimes be just as powerful as the fear of failing. Healing physically and spiritually demands that others expect more from me than I am already giving, and that can be overwhelming and intimidating.

The key then, and still is, to stay calm and focus on grounding, slowly moving one leg at a time, grounding again, and repeating with the other. I must stop holding my breath and just move and breathe while cherishing each and every step. The stage of healing has once again been transforming, and for now it's back to basics saying "thank you" with each and every step I take.

I have experienced every range of emotions since then, and I'm still brought to tears when I think about walking again. That experience has ignited in me a new willingness to go after my healing with a vengeance and give it all I've got.

I have been blessed to know some of the most amazing and strongest people in this world. Many have come and gone.

I am so very thankful for the support I have from Kay Lathrop and her amazing Warriors who have recovered from SCI. They've recovered from what was described as incomplete and complete spinal cord injuries, but didn't let the doctors' negative attitudes influence them to the point where it hindered their recovery for any length of time.

The key for me has been keeping a positive mind, and surrounding myself with people who love and support me. I stop myself in my tracks when I start thinking bad things about what is in store for me.

Even after all this time, when I was standing at ReWalk on my way home from that magnificent day, I quietly found myself thinking in a contaminating way. It was so hard, and it took all I had to complete the walk and not black out. I thought to myself, "OK, you have the experience. Now move on; it was nice but probably not for me."

The following day, after reviewing what I just been through, I'm thinking to myself "Oh my God, now more than ever, I know better! I have to watch the way I think and how I talk to myself!"

I immediately shared with a few fellow Warriors who have recovered or are recovering from complete and incomplete spinal cord injuries. When I said out loud how I was feeling I realized how stupid and self-defeating it was to think that way and to hold those thoughts for too long. Instead, I worked on changing my internal dialogue, and forced myself to focus on all the positive things I have done and have experienced this far without doctors urging me on. I am strong, committed, and determined to prove them all wrong, no matter how long it takes.

> *"As a single footstep will not make a path on earth, so a single thought will not make a pathway in the mind. To make a deep physical path, we walk again and again. To make a deep mental path, we must think over and over the kind of thoughts we wish to dominate our lives."*
> *– Henry David Thoreau*

After my three months of physical and occupational therapy ended I started to feel a bit lost and a little down. That reaction was something I had come to expect and knew would eventually subside once I established a new therapy schedule I could follow on my own at home. The initial fear of not having access to the proper equipment (parallel bars) a set schedule, someone to help me lock my braces and assist with walking could have become overwhelming. It was at this point I needed to revert to what I knew and that was practicing the art of being grateful. I once again would experience a deeper form of gratitude because I was faced with what seemed to be troubled times. Working on mastering the art of being grateful is what always saves me.

Late at night unable to sleep, I found myself lying in bed doing my hand exercises while they rested on my abdomen. No doubt my hands and my functionality had improved during those three months but even knowing that truth, all my old mental movies from the doctors would start to play in my head such as "you will never…" and "if you were ever to walk you first would get back functionality in your hands" I found myself then questioning what their definition of functionality might have been. After having everything stolen from me, functionality took on a whole new meaning. Even the slightest bit of improvement was a plus and always restored my confidence. Quite honestly it really didn't matter anymore. It is a flawed thought process and not one I wanted to feed.

After all, I am the creator of my destiny and my therapy is totally in my hands. That thought can initiate fear or it can liberate, and that night I made a conscious decision to choose liberation over fear! Thinking positive and healing thoughts is where it always starts for me because experiencing wholeness and interconnectedness springs from facing my fears. It's my path to realizing my dreams of stronger hands and increased mobility.

It was on that sleepless night I made a promise to myself that I would be my own best friend and cheerleader, knowing that with every step I took it was a way for me to facilitate my healing at a much deeper level. My gratitude and walking journey is a lifelong commitment that will be accomplished by taking it one day at a time and one step at a time.

Most my healing has come from a myriad of practices which include, but are not limited to, various forms of yoga, meditation, sound healing, and ultimately prayer. I have established my own therapy schedule I follow at home while also utilizing my local resources, where I can swim and stretch on mat tables. Traditional therapies were good as far as they went, but continued recovery for me was found in the "nontraditional" therapies.

My mission for now is to share my story with college students studying Occupational and Physical Therapies. Our current textbooks do not include stories like mine, so I know my job for now is to be that living "textbook". My healing will be a lifelong process, and never have I felt more blessed as I do today!

Don't ask what the world needs. Ask what makes you come alive and go do it. Because what the world needs is people who have come alive.
— Howard Thurman

If you're newly injured, please never give up. Choose your thoughts carefully. After all, half the battle is fought inside of us all, and with right thinking we all have the power to overcome anything.

Thank you for taking time to read my story, sharing in my walking journey with me. I always reach a new understanding once I write things down. It's my hope that your burden has been lessened.

"Get your fire back, it's not over until God says it's over. Start believing again. Start dreaming again. Start pursuing what God put in your heart!"
– Joel Osteen

Chapter 23. *Tips to Make Life Easier, and Things I Wish I Had Done Sooner to Accelerate My Healing*

Bought a set of therapy steps to make transferring onto the floor and back into my chair possible.

Had someone make a smaller transfer board with a handle so that I could transfer myself.

If you have pets, take time to pet them; they are great therapy! I found wanting to scratch our cats has helped me gain more finger and hand function back.

Use adaptive devices sooner, such as a buttonhole hooker, or a hairbrush with a handle.

Zipping anything up was impossible, so we put a key chain ring on all of my zippers so I could at least try it. Because of doing this, I am able to zip most things up and don't ask for help unless it's absolutely necessary.

Don't use elastic shoestrings; keep trying to tie your own shoes even if you are slow and too weak to make a bow. Partially making a bow that becomes untied is better than none at all! Practice makes perfect.

When bending over, do it in front of a bed. When tying my shoes I rest my forehead on the bed. It keeps me in my chair along with providing stability.

I use my standing frame on a daily basis to help strengthen my remaining ab muscles and to improve balance. This has made living life a lot easier!

Lastly, I would recommend NOT getting rid of clothing you think you will never be able to put on yourself. I got rid of a lot of clothing such as belts, jeans, skorts, pocketbooks, jackets with zippers and button down tops thinking "I will never be able to…."

Well, I was wrong, and today I wish I had those items back.

Chapter 24. *Call to Action*

If I could change one thing about the way spinal cord injury is treated, it would be changing the attitudes and beliefs of those who treat us. I was blessed to have been surrounded by a few positive and uplifting women who believed in me and my abilities. Unlike the doctors, they never told me "I would never." Nor was I told "at 18 months you will stop healing."

Thank You All

This has been a learning experience for me, and I am a better individual because of my suffering. The one lesson all of us could work on perfecting is being more careful of the thoughts we hold, how we treat people, and what we say. Attitude is everything, and it can make or break someone's spirit. So, if it doesn't build up, edify, or encourage, don't say it, and immediately work on eliminating it from your life.

I am proof that there is healing even after 18 months. Each of us must be treated as special. There are no rules for recovery. We are each unique and should be treated as such!

Since walking in the suit, I have been given a sense of renewed hope. I am fueled with a determination to push myself, and expect that that experience has incited more healing. My goal from this day forward will be to perfect standing and walking with my KAFO braces.

It seems like only yesterday I walked for the first time in ten and a half years. Attitude and persistence has been my saving grace, and I am committed to reclaiming my proper place in this life. For now my life will consist of OT and PT four days a week, and eventually I will return to work while still being committed to inspiring other SCI patients, offering them hope and another side of the story.

A new milestone was reached recently and I could not be more grateful than I am right now! My PT told me she was not pushing my walker for me and that I was doing it all on my own. Her words were "I am just eye candy."

I awoke this morning and never felt more grateful, and am excited to discover what I can and will accomplish next!

What's my Call to Action?

1. If you have a spinal cord injury, please realize that even though you are in for a serious struggle, your life has value, and you might greatly improve your abilities.

2. Be thankful for what you have, not bitter about what you have lost.

3. Use below-injury massage and exercise to send neural messages upstream to your brain.

4. Strong faith in God or your higher power will help you overcome negative thoughts.

5. Your helpers mean well, but make sure they are letting you try to do things by yourself even though it takes longer.

6. Don't be afraid to change doctors or other health professionals if you feel like they are negative or holding you back.

7. You have a new job now. You have things of your own to overcome and you must also help others to overcome their problems.

So how do I finish my book while I am continuing to heal day by day? I guess now is a good time. I am walking with my KAFO braces with little if any assistance, and will continue to set distance records.

Fortunately, I am able to update my book at almost any time, thanks to modern technology. Plus you can keep up with me on my blog and Facebook page.

Meanwhile, I pray that I have given hope to those of you that are suffering from SCI, or alcohol abuse, or spousal abuse, or any other challenge that you need to overcome. If I can do it, you can, too!

I will respond to as many speaking invitations as I can, because I firmly believe that God has that in His plan for me. I also hope that you will help others as a result of reading my book.

www.shellykerchner.com
https://www.facebook.com/shelly.kerchner

Hello, Wonderful World!

Appendix A: My Poems

Filled with Hope

Filled with hope and anxiousness of things yet to come makes each moment of doubt and fear easier to overcome.
Finding out who you are and what your purpose is makes each moment so much easier to get through.
Not knowing what may unfold at one time left me paralyzed with fear has now become something to be grateful for.
Not knowing what's next or what's in store for me makes each day more precious than ever before.

The Gifts

Every day is a gift when we believe we are exactly where we should be.
Even if you must pretend, that's OK, because eventually it will become your new reality.
Not looking back or even forward but remain in the right here and now.
Yesterday is gone and tomorrow just a dream, so stay in today and make it all that it should be
Today is a gift that's given to all so make it your job to never fall.
Find out what you are called to do and give it your all
So that living life benefits all!

Thank You to My Sponsor

I never had anyone to bounce things off of and never knew that's what healthy people do.
Thank you for being that person and always helping me through.
I've learned how to think things through, no longer second guess everything I do
and now I know how to make rational decisions. I just wanted to take this opportunity to say thank you!

Coping

Keep your head up and stop looking down.
Keep looking around and forging ahead
Today is a new day so start over new
Ask a few questions and having them answered is still so new
This new way to cope is all still brand new
Thankful for all that have been blessed to do and want to say thank you!

Happy, Joyous, and Free
My childhood was filled with dysfunction of every type which left me
feeling isolated and on my own.
Operating under all that fear and tension was never God's intention.
He wants me to be happy, joyous and free of all insecurities.
I am grateful for the realization of this new reality and for the gift of just
being me
What an amazing place to be!

Appendix B: My Journal

July 31 2006 day of my accident.

Oct 2006 Carried out of my house with only my medical equipment and clothes on my back!

Feb 2007 No more bowl baths!! "People who care" bought me a tub transfer bench! Had my first shower!! Felt Amazing!

June 4 2007 put shampoo and conditioner in my hair alone!

March 3 2007 first time to a grocery store!

April 10 2007 first Day of PT with Bruce.

May 22 2007 learned how to sit up and turn on my side!

May 28 2007 Bruce talked to me about being more independent.

June 25 2007 OJ lady at PT "you deserve this more than me!" Never know how god wants to use you!

July 6 2007 TF from chair to toilet, no board and no help!

July 6 2007 TF from mat to chair with no board!

July 9 2007 Christian work camp making doors wider and in and out of house possible!

June 3 2007 washed and dried myself!

June 5 2007 went to the mall in manual chair alone!

June 8 2007 learned moving inch by inch to transfer was ok! Progress not perfection!

June 13 2007 turned on water in shower at mom's by myself!

June 15 2007 flushed the toilet for the first time!

June 25 2009 OJ lady, never know how god wants to use me!

Aug 30 put on sneakers & socks on in my manual chair by myself for the first time!

Sept 22 2007 picked up ice with reacher and blueberries. Didn't get angry, just giggled!

Sept 23 2007 dropped pills, no anger! Picked them up saying thank you while picking each one up with my reacher!

Sept 24 2007 getting closer to God! Always searching, always knocking on god's door. Not knowing I had his love and protection all along!

Oct 5 2007 Thanks for giving me the strength to open Mom's bathroom door, could not do this last month!

October 5 2007 left hand is getting stronger. Bruce did not have to wrap it to the arm bike!

Oct 9 2007 Can turn on my CD player without using my teeth!

Oct 10 2007 tied hair back with a scrunchie that was stretched out!

Oct 30 2007 Dr. Reiter said bone, plate, and screws are healing just wonderfully!

Oct 30 2007 Pulled a magnet off the fridge for the first time!

Nov. 3 2007 Rolled! Was lying on my back and rolled to my side!

Nov. 7 Figured out a way to get my own hot cup of tea using a small tray and dycem (non-slip pad)!

November 11 2007 picked up my own wash cloth in shower!

Nov. 11 2007 able to pick up a coffee pot!

Feb 13 2008 movement in index finger!

Feb 20 2008 opened a milk box!

Feb 21 2008 transfers are getting easier!

Feb 21 2008 did 30 wheelchair pushups!

Feb 25 2008 peeled an egg and an orange, wasn't pretty but I did it!

Feb 28 2008 fell out of chair again!

Feb 29 2008 tied shoes!

March 4 2008 took door adaptive handles off!!!

Aug 24 2008 opened a can of soda!

Aug 25 2008 his lawyer concerned for my safety, unpredictable and angry.

Sept 9 2008 Mom was robbed.

Oct 2009 forced to spend 1 hour 10 min in a cold dirty bathroom at the transit station, remained strong!

Oct 12 2009 Accept, adjust, move on, fight. Resist being discouraged! Trouble in bathroom between classes.

Oct 22 2009 feeling renewed!

Oct 31 2009 Only constant in this world is God's love, protection, and care!

Nov 6 2009 learning to control my feelings, overwhelmed in computer class, hands frustrating!

Nov 8 2009 God gave me the gift of grace to love and protect myself.

Nov 30 2009 wheelchair broke down -- I didn't!

Nov 31 2009 Trust God, trust myself, then trust others!

Jan 20 2009 first day at the community college, Obama was sworn in.

Feb 9 2009 folded my white blanket!

Jan 19 2008 Jill took me to HGA (His Glory Alone).

Jan 23 2008 switched from manual to electric chair.

Feb 5 2008 Taking things month to month!

August 2007 got up onto my hands and knees!

Jan 17 2008 last day of therapy with Bruce!

Jan 22 2008 buttoned five buttons in 15 minutes!

Jan 20, 2009 First day of community college.

April 24 2008 Hernia removed.

July 11 2008 changed my own cushion cover!

July 31, 2008 two years in chair!

August 15 2008 first time out to eat at home.

June 09 2009 first transfer into a booth while out to eat.

June 24, 2009 the bus incident with the drunk lady, god working real time!

July 3 2009 first visit home. Mom was drinking I didn't. Went to my first AA meeting back home.

July 10, 2009 Was able to peel my own shrimp!

July 10 2009 Got my acceptance level from UPJ! (University of Pittsburg at Johnstown).

July 14 2009 Started facing all my insecurities.

July 19 2009 Went downtown by myself to Johnstown Flood Memorial.

July 21 2009 run through with Jan (OT) to ensure room was accessible.

July 23 2009 Patti took me to my first AA meeting, in my manual chair; went for ice cream!

July 23 2009 Conflict with Personal Care Agency; warned I would lose them if I didn't use them.

July 27 2009 picked up my books from UPJ.

JULY 27 2009 Put on teds myself and dressed alone only took 45 minutes.

August 8 2009 Opened my bedroom door with my left hand!

August 8 2009 changing channels on the remote is getting easier!

August 10 2009 last walk-through in room at UPJ with Jane.

August 6 2009 making waves, changed personal care agency.

August 12 2009 Fred and June helped me start moving onto campus!

August 16, came out to Mom again. She was fine with it.

August 21 2009 last night at HGA.

August 22 first morning at UPJ.

Sept 1 2009 first day of 1 semester!

Sept 7 couldn't get into engineering and science building, had to ask for help.

Sept 24 2009 got onto the toilet backwards!

Sept 24 2009 questioning if I need so many hours again, becoming more and more independent!

Oct 18 2009 Worried about Mom.

October 23 first time I swam & didn't sink! Freedom!!

Nov. 7 2009 Learning is fun, love it here!

Nov 30 2009 everyone was concerned about me being alone.

Dec 2 2009 Chair broke down, I didn't!

Aug 31 2010 classes started again at UPJ.

Sept 1 2010 and we are off again!

Sept 7 2010 Slow down, if I don't discipline myself someone or something will. It's a whole a lot easier doing it myself.

Sept 6 2010 I need a goal, or I get down. Keep on keepin' on!

Sept 18 Thank you for all the people you put in my life to help love, guide & protect me.

Sept 18 2010 it's not about having what you want, it's wanting what you've got!

Sept 20 2010 doing laundry, locked myself out, didn't break down!

Sept 21 Reported aide for stealing.

Sept 30 2010 cannot operate my chair and hold an umbrella without the wind taking it, too weak. Got soaked!

Sept 30 2010 stop allowing others to drain me!

Oct 2 2010 went to the ball field and into the bathroom and just screamed, letting off tension! Felt great!

OCT 5 2010- THERE IS A SOLUTION TO EVERY PROBLEM I MUST BE CREATIVE ENOUGH TO FIGURE ONE OUT!

October 10 2010 my letter was published in New Mobility magazine "Post Traumatic Growth is Alive and Well."

Oct 15 2010 Range of motion is better, was able to wash my back and arms! Thank you!

Oct 21 2010 wheelchair dancing, did the tango! Nov 8 2010 took 3 4 minutes to put on my pillow case, first time!

Nov 2010 Started UPJ Thank You Day for the kids!!

NOV 12 2010 BOUGHT MY FIRST PAIR OF JEANS AND PUT THEM ON BY MYSELF!

Nov 16 2010 hung a shirt up for the first time, used my left hand to hang it up!

Nov 25 2010 asked for a sign, butterflies on my chair handle and landed on my left knee 4 times, stopped counting after that. Amazing!

Nov 29 2010 no longer need the adaptive hairbrush (with the Velcro) thank you for continued healing!

Jan 14 2011 signed lease for apartment, moving again!

July 2014 Could only lift 3 cat bowls w/ left hand.

July 8, 2015 I can lift all 9 cat dishes with my left hand. Started chair yoga again!

2016

July 7 While tying my shoes I realized I have my strength on my fingers and hands, last year I could barely make a bow much less pull my strings tight!

July 31 - my 10-year anniversary!

Aug 27 stood for the first time with my walker (no braces), once outside then two times off the bed! Feeling powerful and full of hope again!

Aug 28 Tried to stand at Planet Fitness and spasmed then whacked my head on a metal bar, resulting in my first black eye!

Aug 29 Stood with my new walker for 7 minutes in increments of 3 min, then 1.

Also got fitted for my braces, not a complex process at all! I may have them in a few days!

Aug 30 PT today stood 4 min twice then 3 minutes.

Deep muscle massage with Shari, afterwards she told me to push with my heels AND I DID!!

(Anxiously awaiting the arrival of my braces). Anyone who claims braces are cumbersome has never been confined to wheelchair or has not gone any amount of time without being mobile. So excited to get them.

Aug 31 PT today stood four minutes, another four, then three minutes.

Sept 6 Got my AFO braces today have concerns they're not going to help me, I'm still bending of the knee maybe PT can help.

September 9, 2016 just left PT stayed for the first time with my Braces and Walker hear it was a struggle but I won't quit it's hard but makes it easier a little.

Monday, September 12, 2016 put braces on today alone for the second time, then stood in my standing frame for a half an hour.

September 13, 2016 Stood with braces for 15 seconds there's more exercise of my legs instead of upper body.

September 16, 2016 stood six times from the mat table, with the help of my walker.

September 19, 2016 went from the mat to standing 40+ times with the help of the Walker.

September 20, 2016, I can take two steps back when getting into position to sit down.

And I figured out a way to stand alone in front of my bed with my walker and braces, by transferring going to bed adding another cushion on to my wheelchair, transfer back into it. From there I am up higher so it's easier to stand directly from the chair.

September 2016 stood at the parallel bars with my AFO braces with the assistance of three people.

Stood five times at home alone with my walker. I used the bed to stabilize my walker, without much of a struggle.

October 3, 2016 stood at PT at 19 1/4 inches! Four weeks ago it was 22 inches. I am making progress.

Wednesday, October 5, 2016 Physical Therapy said I've mastered standing from mat table so the chairs next also stood in PT 40 times from various heights.

Monday, October 24 2016 enjoyed speaking at North Star high school.

November 2, 2016 While standing today my heels were only off the floor a ¼ inch instead of one inch, progress!

December 9, 2016 Released from PT.

2017

January 16, 2017 Dr. FINALLY agreed that I need KAFO braces (Knee, Ankle, Foot Orthosis).

January 18 Got down on the floor today, used my therapy steps to get down. Successfully was able to get up on all fours and balance myself quadruped. Also did rolling.

February 8 another milestone, stood for two minutes today, started working on my book.

February 10 fitted for my KAFO braces.

February 12 typing is better with my left hand.

January 14, I can hold a bottle of soda in my left hand and pour it without dropping it.

February 22 Met with my new doctor at UPMC hospital. I like her! She wrote me a script for gait training in PT.

February 23 I can put my hands behind my back while in the shower without the fear of toppling over!!

February 27 start visualizing moving my toes and ankles once more and had some movement.

March 1 I can put my hands on my hips while I'm in my standing frame without falling over.

March 17 still writing a book.

March 20 I can tear two layers of paper last year I struggled to tear one piece!

March 22 it's easier to bend over and tie my shoes since I've been standing. I no longer need the bed to prop my head and keep me in the chair.

My pinch is improving! I'm able to hold a shirt sleeve when putting on my jacket.

March 24 pulled a label off a sugar box, I have better dexterity in my index finger and thumb.

March 25 Two times this week I have opened a bottle of soda without dicem. Thank you for the strength in my hands.

March 26 I opened a can of tuna with my manual can opener and without the dicem!

Have been standing at least a half an hour a day, usually one hour a day.

March 30 Picked up my KAFO braces and stood in my frame 1/2 hour.

April 17 I took my first steps today!

6 feet, 10 feet, 7 feet, then 25.

I wish someone would've been there to videotape it!

April 24 Got arm strengthening exercises at occupational therapy.

April 25 had Physical Therapy. Got up on my hands and knees and did push-ups. And got some ab strengthening exercises.

April 27 Occupational therapy working hard. I now have a grip exerciser and therapy putty to work on my left hand at home.

April 28, Today I walked 7 feet, 8 feet instead for three minutes at parallel bars.

April 29 I feel healing taking place in my feet with all kinds of new sensations.

May 2 I got my new chair. Walking is so much easier with my elevating seat. Walked 12 feet, 10, then 20 feet and another 20 feet.

May - started online mindfulness training.

May 4, opened a jar spaghetti sauce without the dicem. I can hold a frying pan with my left hand and clean it out without the fear of dropping it.

May 5 walked 20, 18, 22, 24, and 12 feet.

May 6 open a bag of pretzels without dicem.

May 9 walked 20 feet, 28 with one rest while standing, then 30 feet without stopping.

May 11 I'm having new spasms in my feet and ankles.

I consent ....

May 12 decided not to return my new chair with elevating seat.

Also walked in Physical Therapy 25 feet, 32 feet, 21 feet and then finally 36 feet. Also stood for two minutes three times.

May 13 never a dull moment I was stuck outside in my wheelchair for over an hour.

May 21, 2017 just realize my brace is bent, disappointed because I will have no PT for two entire weeks.

Thursday, May 25 I used my index finger to pull my zipper up first time in 11 years!

After three weeks of no PT:

Friday, June 9 stood at the parallel bars for three minutes, and then two minutes.

Walked 22, 23, 25, then 28 feet.

My PT, Wendy told me she's no longer pushing the walker, she's just eye candy!

It took three times up on my feet before the tingling in my muscle spasms started. Happy that it is returned.

June 12 I'm able to open a can with the pull-tab.

I have the strength in my hands to turn down the sheets with my left hand!

June 13 walked 25, 27 and then 28 feet!

June 16 one month of meditating on a daily basis and I definitely am reaping the benefits.

I walked at PT 22 feet, 24, 22, then 30. And that was after standing two times. Once for three minutes and then for one and a half minutes.

June 20 walked 12 feet, 10, 10, and then finally 20. Just going to call it an off day.

June 24 walked 13, 12, 17 and 16 feet after standing 3 mins twice.

June 27 my PT Wendy is finally back. I walk 20 feet, 17, 21, and 26 feet

June 30 walked 25 feet, 24 feet, 20 feet, and 28 feet.

July 1 picked up a 2-pound box of sugar with my left hand, could hold it long enough and tightly enough to pour a teaspoon of it into my coffee. Left hand is healing.

July 5 appointment in Pittsburgh with Dr. Harrington. Had extensive testing. Neurogenic bladder evaluation at UPMC.

First time this was done in 11 years. This needs to be done once a year!

July 6 walked 20, 15, 25, 26 feet and stood 2 ½ min and then 3 mins.

July 10 loading and unloading the dishwasher is easier. I can grab a handful of silverware at once and pick up plates without thinking "don't drop it".

July 17 set a record! I walked 30 feet, 20 feet, 35 feet and then 38 feet!

Appendix C: My Walking Record

Date	Feet Walked	Longest	Total Feet	Standing
4/17/2017	6, 10, 7	10	23	
5/2/2017	12, 10, 20, 20	20	62	
5/5/2017	20, 18, 22, 24, 12	24	96	
5/9/2017	22, 23, 25, 28	28	98	
5/9/2017	20, 28, 30	30	78	
5/12/2017	25, 32, 21, 36	36	114	2 MIN X 3
6/13/2017	25, 27, 28	28	75	2 MIN 50 SEC
6/16/2017	22, 24, 22, 30	30	98	
6/20/2017	12, 10, 10, 20	20	52	3 MIN
6/24/2017	13, 12, 17, 16	18	58	3 MIN X 2
6/27/2017	20, 17, 21, 26	26	84	
6/30/2017	25, 24, 20, 28	28	97	
7/6/2017	20, 15, 25, 26	26	86	
7/7/2017	30, 20, 35, 38	38	123	
7/11/2017	20, 19, 33, 40, 41	41	153	8 MIN
7/14/2017	48, 38, 38, 47, 26	48	197	9 MIN 30	navigated to corners!
7/18/2017	46, 34, 42, 58	58	180	

133

7/21/2017	39, 42, 50, 57	57	188	step through is improving!
7/26/2017	43, 50, 42, 38	50	163	NO BINDER/AND WITH SKIS
7/29/2017	16, 14, 17, 27, 15, 13	27	102	fighting a cold
9/1/2017	22, 43, 28, 56	56	149	

Appendix D: Social Deviance

Sociologists define deviance as behavior that violates an essential social norm. Individuals who cross over the limits of what is socially acceptable behavior are considered deviant. The term deviance is relative because what is considered deviant behavior in one place may be acceptable in another place. For example, some individuals consider anorexia a deviant behavior. Anorexia involves food restriction and self-starvation, and is characterized by specific personality traits combined with obsessive compulsive behavior. This behavior encompasses preoccupation with food, counting calories and exercising.

This is my personal account of life as an anorexic and a description of my functioning within this closed society for duration of four months. The eating disorder clinic was located in Baltimore, Maryland at Johns Hopkins Hospital. There were unspoken rules to conform to and we shared a comradery because we were of the same mind set. Ultimately our goal was to protect one another from anyone outside our group.

Competition was evident between the girls in regards to who was the thinnest and a hierarchy was formed on that basis. The thinnest individual was granted respect and held authority over the group. With her gray skin tone, fine body hair growth, sunken eyes and slowed motor movements, society would label her weak and frail, but to her peers she was a representation of strength, stability, and security. Her intravenous IV was a symbol of power, authority and incredible display self-discipline to the other girls. She was held in high esteem.

Meal times had duration of one hour, and anyone remaining at the table after the allotted time was escorted to seclusion until her meal was consumed. We protected one another, especially at mealtimes, and working as a unit was a necessity. We would take turns with distracting the supervising nurse in order to successfully dispose of food.

Each patient was assigned a primary nurse upon the day of admission and it was her responsibility to document all issues pertaining to the eating disorder. There was an individual named Grace who consistently spent one hour in seclusion as a result of her eating rituals. Grace would not eat a bite of food until all of her food was cut up in small pieces and then re-arranged in the same positions on her plate. Meat was positioned at twelve o'clock, vegetables at four and rice or pasta at eight o'clock. Grace would take a bite of food then place the silverware down and proceeded to chew each piece of food exactly twenty five times. She would take another bite and the ritual began again. Grace's logic for this ritual was that the number two and the number five added up to seven. To Grace the number seven represented completion. Thus Grace consistently spent a total of two hours until her meals were completed.

After meal times, there was supervision for a total of two hours. This was to prevent elimination of food. If anyone needed to use the restroom we were escorted, and were required to keep the bathroom door ajar. This time period was diminished as we gained weight. We were also told that at any time of the night we would be monitored to also prevent excessive exercising.

Every morning the doctor and nurses would make rounds and evaluate our progress or lack of it. We felt special and for once in our lives we were attracting attention. If asked, each girl would tell you for the first time they felt like they were in control and secure. Anyone who threatened that security was an enemy.

Most anorexics would gain enough weight to be released but immediately would return to starvation or change addictions. If one was anorexic she usually left bulimic and vice versa. Recovery meant no longer having control over our lives, thus the reason for the switch from one destructive behavior to another.

After speaking to another patient a few years ago, we recounted our experience and both agree that Grace still represents power, strength, and security. Today the term deviant can also be used to describe Grace. She was defiant and ultimately that deviance took her life.

Appendix E: I Am

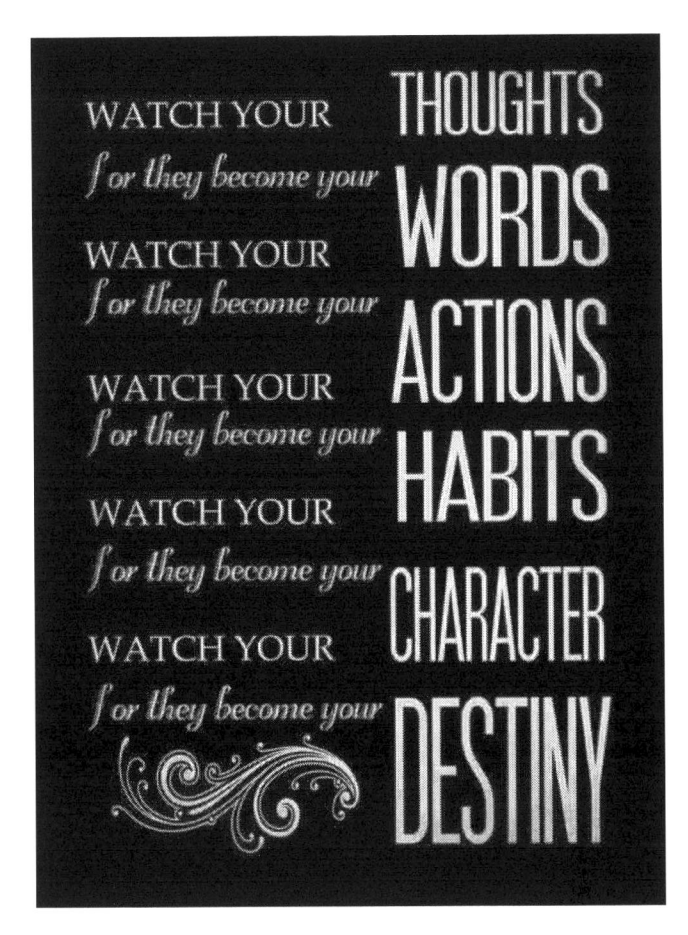

WATCH YOUR **THOUGHTS**
for they become your
WATCH YOUR **WORDS**
for they become your
WATCH YOUR **ACTIONS**
for they become your
WATCH YOUR **HABITS**
for they become your
WATCH YOUR **CHARACTER**
for they become your
DESTINY

I AM A CHILD OF GOD.

1 JOHN 3:1

See what sort of love the Father has given to us: that we should be called God's children and indeed we are! For this reason the world does not know us: because it did not know him.

I AM LOVED

JOHN 3:16

"For God so loved the world that he gave his one and only Son, that whoever believes in him shall not perish but have eternal life.

JOHN 13:34

A new command I give you: Love one another. As I have loved you, so you must love one another.

JOHN 15:9

"As the Father has loved me, so have I loved you. Now remain in my love.

JOHN 15:12

My command is this: Love each other as I have loved you.

I AM PROTECTED

I AM NEVER ALONE.

JOHN 14:16

And I will pray the Father, and He will give you another Helper, that He may abide with you forever

JOSUHA 1:9

I am determined and confident. I am not afraid or discouraged for the Lord God is with me wherever I go.

PASLM 91:11

For He orders His angels to protect you wherever you go.

John 16:7 GOD GAVE US THE HOLY SPIRIT

7Nevertheless I tell you the truth; It is expedient for you that I go away: for if I go not away, the Comforter will not come unto you; but if I depart, I will send him unto you.

GOD GAVE ME THE HOLY SPIRIT EPHESIANS 1:13-14

In Him you also, after listening to the message of truth, the gospel of your salvation having also believed you were sealed in Him with the Holy Spirit of promise. (sealed indicated possession and security of His salvation) I am secure!

GOD GAVE US ANGELS TO HELP US. HEBREWS 13:2

2Do not forget to entertain strangers, for by so doing some people have entertained angels without knowing it.

HEBREWS 13:5

Let your conduct be without covetousness; be content with such things as you have. For He Himself has said, "I will never leave you nor forsake you.

JAMES 4:7

7Submit yourselves, then, to God. Resist the devil, and he will flee from you.

ut knowing it.

MATTHEW 28:19-20

"Go therefore and make disciples of all nations, baptizing them in the name of the Father and the Son and the Holy Spirit. 20Teaching them to observe all that I commanded you; and lo, I am with you always, even to the end of the age."

EPHESIANS 6:13-14

For this reason, take up the full armor of God so that you may be able to stand your ground on the evil day, and having done everything, to stand. 6:14 Stand firm therefore, by fastening the belt of truth around your waist, by putting on the breastplate of righteousness,

JOSHUA 1:5

No man shall be able to stand before you all the days of your life; as I was with Moses, so I will be with you. I will not leave you nor forsake you.

JOSHUA 1:9

Have I not commanded you? Be strong and of good courage; do not be afraid, nor be dismayed, for the LORD your God is with you wherever you go."

GENESIS 28:15

I am with you! I will protect you wherever you go and will bring you back to this land. I will not leave you until I have done what I promised you!"

I AM GROWING

JAMES 1:12

Happy is the one who endures testing, because when he has proven to be genuine, he will receive the crown of life that God promised to those who love him.

I AM STRONG

PHILIPIANS 4:13

I am able to do all things through the one who strengthens me.

2 CORINITHIANS 12:10

That is why, for Christ's sake, I delight in weaknesses, in insults, in hardships, in persecutions, in difficulties. For when I am weak, then I am strong.

EPHESIANS 6:10

10Finally, be strong in the Lord and in his mighty power.

1 CORINITHIANS 10:13

.God is faithful He will keep the temptation from becoming so strong that you can't stand up against. When you are tempted, He will show you a way out so that you will not give in to it.

I AM WISE

JAMES 1:5-8

1:5 But if anyone is deficient in wisdom, he should ask God, who gives to all generously and without reprimand, and it will be given to him.5If any of you lacks wisdom, he should ask God, who gives generously to all without finding fault, and it will be given to him. 6But when he asks, he must believe and not doubt, because he who doubts is like a wave of the sea, blown and tossed by the wind. 7That man should not think he will receive anything from the Lord; 8he is a double-minded man, unstable in all he does

MATTHEW 7:24

Everyone who hears these words of mine and does them is like a wise man who built his house on rock.

PSALM 51:6

Behold, You desire truth in the inward parts, And in the hidden part You will make me to know wisdom

PSALM 107:43

Whoever is wise will observe these things, And they will understand the loving kindness of the LORD.

PSALM 119:98

Thy commandments make me wiser than my enemies, for they are ever mine.

EPHESIANS 1:17

That the God of our Lord Jesus Christ which, the Father of glory, may give you a spirit of wisdom and of revelation in the knowledge of Him.

PROVERBS 28:7

Keep the law of God and man and I am wise.

I AM PROTCTED

PASLMS 91:11

For He orders His angels to protect you wherever you go.

I Eph 6:10   The protection for believers

Finally, be strengthened in the Lord and in the strength of his power.

Put on righteousness Again, know who I am in Christ. Stop feeling bad about myself. God will provide for me.

I AM CONFIDENT

PSALM 31:24

Be strong and confident, all you who wait on the Lord.

I AM BRAVE

JOSHUA 1:9

I repeat, be strong and brave! Don't be afraid and don't panic, for I, the Lord your God, am with you in all you do."

I AM VALUABLE

MATTHEW 10:31

So do not be afraid; you are more valuable than many sparrows.

I AM FILLED WITH POWER WITH THE SPIRIT OF THE LORD

MICAH 3:8

But as for me, I am filled with power, with the Spirit of the LORD, and with justice and might, to declare to Jacob his transgression, to Israel his sin. (Ask God to fill me with His power!)

EPHESIANS 3:16

That He would grant you, according to the riches of His glory, to be strengthened with power through His spirit in the inner man.

I AM HOLY

1 PETER 1:16

for it is written, "You shall be holy, because I am holy."

LEVITICUS 11:44

I am the Lord your God, consecrate yourselves and be Holy because I am holy. Do not make yourselves unclean by any creature that moves.

EPHESIANS 1:4

Just as He chose us in Him before the foundation of the world, that we should be holy and blameless before Him in love.

I AM ABOVE NOT BENEATH

I AM THE HEAD NOT THE TAIL

DETUTERONMY 28:13

The Lord will make you the head and not the tail, and you will always end up at the top and not at the bottom, if you obey his commandments which I am urging you today to be careful to do.

I AM COMPLETE (SATISIFIED)

I AM SECURE

COLOSSIANS 3:10

And in Him you have been made complete.

I AM BLESSED

GENESIS 12:2

I will make you into a great nation and I will bless you; I will make your name great, and you will be a blessing.

JAMES 1:22-25

But be sure you live out the message and do not merely listen to it and so deceive yourselves. 1:23 For if someone merely listens to the message and does not live it out, he is like someone who gazes at his own face in a mirror. 1:24 For he gazes at himself and then goes out and immediately forgets what sort of person he was. 1:25 But the one who peers into the perfect law of liberty and fixes his attention there, and does not become a forgetful listener but one who lives it out – he will be blessed in what he does

JAMES 1:12 Blessed is the man who perseveres under trial, because when he has stood the test, he will receive the crown of life that God has promised to those who love him.

PSALM 84:12 (KJV)

Blessed is the man that trusteth in Thee.

PSALM 1:1

How blessed is the one who does not follow the advice of the wicked,

LIFE IS FULL OF TESTS

JAMES 1:2-3

Consider it all joy, my brethren when you encounter various trials, knowing that the testing of your faith produces endurance.

God is faithful He will keep the temptation from becoming so strong that you can't stand up against. When you are tempted, He will show you a way out so that you will not give in to it. God is faithful

God does not want me to run from my problems. If I do I will have to confront it again and again and again…

I AM BLESSED

JAMES 1:12

God Blesses the people who patiently endure testing. Afterward they will receive the crown of life that God has promised to those who love Him

EPHESIANS 1:3

3Praise be to the God and Father of our Lord Jesus Christ, who has blessed us in the heavenly realms with every spiritual blessing in Christ.

GENESIS 12:2

I will make you a great nation; I will bless you And make your name great; And you shall be a blessing.

1PETER 3:9 - 10

9Do not repay evil with evil or insult with insult, but with blessing, because to this you were called so that you may inherit a blessing.10For, "Whoever would love life and see good days must keep his tongue from evil and his lips from deceitful speech.

I AM THE RIGHTEOUSNESS OF GOD

2 CORINITHIANS 5:21

God made Him who had no sin to be sin for us, so that in Him we might become the righteousness of God.

ROMANS 1:17

For the righteousness of God is revealed in the gospel from faith to faith, just as it is written, "The righteous by faith will live."

I AM FREE FROM THE LAW OF SIN AND DEATH

ROMANS 8:2

For the law of the life-giving Spirit in Christ Jesus has set you free from the law of sin and death.

I AM CONTENT

PHILIPIANS 4:4-13 - Freedom from care or discomfort

CONTENTMENT 4:4-13

4Rejoice in the Lord always. I will say it again: Rejoice! 5Let your gentleness be evident to all. The Lord is near. 6Do not be anxious about anything, but in everything, by prayer and petition, with thanksgiving, present your requests to God. 7And the peace of God, which transcends all understanding, will guard your hearts and your minds in Christ Jesus. 8Finally, brothers, whatever is true, whatever is noble, whatever is right, whatever is pure, whatever is lovely, whatever is admirable—if anything is excellent or praiseworthy—think about such things. 9Whatever you have learned or received or heard from me, or seen in me—put it into practice. And the God of peace will be with you.

HEBREWS 13:5

Let your conduct be without covetousness; be content with such things as you have. For He Himself has said, "I will never leave you nor forsake you.

Thanks for Their Gifts

10I rejoice greatly in the Lord that at last you have renewed your concern for me. Indeed, you have been concerned, but you had no opportunity to show it. 11I am not saying this because I am in need, for I have learned to be content whatever the circumstances. 12I know what it is to be in need, and I know what it is to have plenty. I have learned the secret of being content in any and every situation, whether well fed or hungry, whether living in plenty or in want. 13I can do everything through him who gives me strength.

DEMONSTRATE GOD'S LOVE

PHILIPIANS 4:5

Let your forbearing spirit be known to all men

Forbear means vi hold back from something: to not do or say something that you could do or say, especially when this shows self-control or consideration for the feelings of others I forbore to criticize their efforts, though criticism was well deserved.

vti be tolerant: to tolerate something with patience or endurance willing to forbear their failures

Old English forberan , literally "bear against

GOD IS PLEASED WITH ME!

PSALM 147:11

The Lord is pleased with those who worship Him and trust His love.

I AM GOD'S SERVANT

MATTHEW 20:27-28

27And whoever wants to be first among you must be your slave. 28 Just as the Son of Man did not did not come to be served but to serve, and to give His life as a ransom for many.

2 CORITHIANS 6:4

4Rather, as servants of God we commend ourselves in every way: in great endurance; in troubles, hardships and distresses.

ROMANS 6:16 (KJV)

16Know ye not, that to whom ye yield yourselves servants to obey, his servants ye are to whom ye obey; whether of sin unto death, or of obedience unto righteousness?

We can obey God or obey Satan.

ROMANS 12:10, 11

Be devoted to one another in brotherly love; give preference to one another in honor; not lagging in diligence, fervent in serving the Lord;

MATTHEW 20:28

just as the Son of Man did not come to be served but to serve, and to give his life as a ransom 39 for many."

1CHRONICLES 28:9

"As for you, my son Solomon, know the God of your father, and serve Him with a whole heart and a willing mind; for the Lord searches all hearts, and understands every intent of the thoughts. If you seek Him, He will let you find Him; but if you forsake Him, He will reject you forever.

I AM NOT AFRAID

JOSHUA 1:9

I repeat, be strong and brave! Don't be afraid and don't panic, for I, the Lord your God, am with you in all you do

2 TIMOYHY 1:7

God did not give me a spirit of fear and timidity but one of power, love and self-discipline.

I AM MERCIFUL

HEBREWS 4:16

Let us therefore draw near with confidence to the throne of grace. That we may receive mercy and may find grace to help in time of need.

I AM THE HOME OF GOD

EPHESIANS 3:16-21

3:17 that Christ may dwell in your hearts through faith, so that, because you have been rooted and grounded in love, 3:18 you may be able to comprehend with all the saints what is the breadth and length and height and depth, 3:19 and thus to know the love of Christ that surpasses knowledge, so that you may be filled up to all the fullness of God.

I AM SANCTIFIED

1 CORINITHIANS 6:8

But you were washed, you were sanctified, you were justified in the name of the Lord Jesus Christ and by the Spirit of our God.

I AM CONFIDENT

PSALM 31:24

Be strong and confident, all you who wait on the Lord

PHILIPIANS 3:3

For we are the circumcision, who worship in the spirit of God and glory in Christ Jesus and put no confidence in the flesh,

I AM COURAGEOUS

JOSHUA 1:9

Have I not commanded you? Be strong and courageous. Do not be terrified; do not be discouraged, for the LORD your God will be with you wherever you go."

DEUTERONOMY 31:6 (NKJV)

I am strong and of good courage, I do not fear nor am I afraid, for the Lord my God, He is the one who goes with me. He will not leave me nor forsake me.

I AM JOYFUL JOHN 10:10

The thief comes only to steal and kill and destroy; I have come that they may have life, and have it to the full.

JOHN 15:11

I have told you this so that my joy may be in you and that your joy may be complete.

JOHN 16:24

Until now you have not asked for anything in my name. Ask and you will receive, and your joy will be complete.

JOHN 17:13

13"I am coming to you now, but I say these things while I am still in the world, so that they may have the full measure of my joy within them.

PSALM 16:10

11 You have made [e] known to me the path of life; you will fill me with joy in your Presence, with eternal pleasures at your right hand.

1 CHRONICLES 16:27

Honor and majesty are {found} in His presence; strength and joy are {found} in His sanctuary.

I AM LOVING

I AM PEACEFUL - Untroubled by conflict, agitation or connotation

I AM PATIENT - Bearing pains or trials calmly or without complaint

I AM KIND

I AM HUMBLE- Not proud or haughty (blatantly and disdainfully proud.) not arrogant (feeling or showing self-importance and contempt or disregard for others)

I AM GOOD

I AM FAITHFUL

Steadfast in affection or allegiance

I AM GENTLE

I POSSESS SELF DISIPLINE

I AM COMPASSIONATE

I AM FORGIVING

GALATIONS 5:22-23

22But the fruit of the Spirit is love, joy, peace, patience, kindness, goodness, faithfulness, 23gentleness and self-control. Surrender to the Holy Spirit and I will have these.

I AM PEACEFUL, UNTROUBLED BY CONFLICT, AGITATION OR CONNOTATION.

COL 3:12-13

I AM PATIENT, I BEAR TRIALS WITHOUT COMPLAINT

12Therefore, as God's chosen people, holy and dearly loved, clothe yourselves with compassion, kindness, humility, gentleness and patience. 13Bear with each other and forgive whatever grievances you may have against one another. Forgive as the Lord forgave you. 14And over all these virtues put on love, which binds them all together in perfect unity

I AM FORGIVING

EPHESIANS 4:23

Be kind and compassionate to one another, forgiving each other, just as in Christ God forgave you.

ASK GOD TO RENEW MY MIND DAILY FORGIVING EW MY MIND DAILY! EPHESIANS 4:23

And that you be renewed in the spirit of your mind. To be made new in the attitude of your minds.

I BELONG TO GOD

PSALM 24:1

The Lord owns the earth and all it contains, the world and all who live

I HAVE ENDURANCE

1 CORINITHIANS 10:13

No trial has overtaken you that is not faced by others. And God is faithful: He will not let you be tried beyond what you are able to bear, but with the trial will also provide a way out so that you may be able to endure it.

I HAVE SELF DISIPLINE

2 TIMOTHY 1:7

For God did not give us a Spirit of fear but of power and love and self-control

GODS POWER IS IN ME

EPHISIANS 1:19-23

of his immense strength. 1:20 This power he exercised in Christ when he raised him from the dead and seated him at his right hand in the heavenly realms 1:21 far above every rule and authority and power and dominion and every name that is named, not only in this age but also in the one to come. 1:22 And God put all things under Christ's feet, and he gave him to the church as head over all things. 1:23 Now the church is his body, the fullness of him who fills all in all.

I HAVE POWER AND AUTHORITY OVER SATAN

LUKE 10:19

Look, I have given you authority to tread on snakes and scorpions and on the full force of the enemy, and nothing will hurt you.

THE HOLY SPIRIT LIVES WITHIN ME

LUKE 11:13

If you then, although you are evil, know how to give good gifts to your children, how much more will the heavenly Father give the Holy Spirit to those who ask him!"

MAKE LOVING GOD & SERVING GOD MY #1 PURPOSE AND HE WILL TAKE CARE OF EVERYTHING ELSE.

ROMANS 8:12

And we know that in all things God works for the good of those who love him, who have been called according to his purpose.

I AM GOD'S SERVANT

1 CORINITHIANS 12:6

"God works through different people in different ways, but it is the same God who achieves His purpose through them all".

2 CORITHIANS 6:4

Rather, as servants of God we commend ourselves in everyway; in great endurance; in troubles, hardships and distresses.

I AM LOVED

PSALM 59:17

You are my source of strength! I will sing praises to you! For God is my refuge, the God who loves me.

EPHESIANS 2:4,5

But God, being rich in mercy, because of His great love with which He loved us, even when we were dead in our transgressions, made us alive together with Christ

I WAS CHOSEN BY GOD!

Elect means chosen by God: people believed to be specially chosen or favored by God, e.g. those chosen by God for salvation

JOHN 5:16

16You did not choose me, but I chose you and appointed you to go and bear fruit—fruit that will last. Then the Father will give you whatever you ask in my name.

I AM HOLY

I AM LOVED

beloved means someone who is loved very much!

I AM MEEK

enduring injury with patience and without resentment

I AM FORGIVING

I AM PATIENT

bearing pains or trials calmly or without complaint

I AM HUMBLE - Not proud or haughty; not arrogant or assertive. HAUGHTY means blantly and disdainfully proud.

(ROMANS 12:16 Be of the same mind toward one another; do not be HAUGHTY in mind, but associate with the lowly. Do not be wise in your own estimation.)

I AM KIND

COLOSSIANS 3:12-13

Therefore, as the elect of God, holy and beloved, put on tender mercies, kindness, humility, meekness, longsuffering (patiently enduring lasting offense or hardship) 13bearing (the manner in which one bears or comports oneself) with one another, and forgiving one another, if anyone has a complaint against another; even as Christ forgave you. So you also must do.

GOD CHOSE ME

EPHESIANS 1:4

Just as He chose us in Him before the foundation of the world.

I AM HOLY

That we should be holy and blameless before Him

I AM LED BY THE SPIRIT

Galatians 5:16-17

16This I say then, Walk in the Spirit, and ye shall not full-fill the lust of the flesh.

17For the flesh lusteth against the Spirit, and the Spirit against the flesh: and these are contrary the one to the other: so that ye cannot do the things that ye would. But I say to you walk by the spirit and you will not carry out the desire of the flesh.

COLOSSIANS 2:5-6

2:5 For though I am absent from you in body, I am present with you in spirit, rejoicing to see your morale and the firmness of your faith in Christ.

Warnings Against the Adoption of False Philosophies

2:6 Therefore, just as you received Christ Jesus as Lord, continue to live your lives in him, rooted and built up in him and firm in your faith just as you were taught, and overflowing with thankfulness.

I AM COMPLETE

COLOSSIANS 3:10   COMPLETE = SATISIFIED

And in him you have been made complete, and He is the head over all rule and authority.

I AM THANKFUL

THESESSALONIANS 5:18

In everything give thanks; for this is God's will for you in Christ Jesus.

GOD HAS A PLAN FOR ME!

JERIMIAH 29:11

For I know the plans that I have for you, declares the Lord, plans for welfare and not for calamity to give you a future and a hope.

EPHESIANS 1:5 (NLT)

"His unchanging plan has always been to adopt us into His own family by bringing us to Himself through Jesus Christ.

I DO NOT HAVE TO WORK AT GOD'S PLAN FOR ME, HE WILL CAUSE IT TO COME TO PASS PHILIPIANS 1:6.

For I am confident of his very thing that he who began a good work in you will perfect it until the day of Jesus Christ.

PRAY BOLD AGGRESSIVE PRAYERS!

HEBREWS 4:16

Let us fearlessly and confidently and boldly draw near to the throne of grace. That we may receive mercy and find grace to help in good time for every need.

PROVERBS 4:23

Watch over your heart with all diligence, for from it flow the springs of life.

LEARN TO APPLY THE WORD TO MY LIFE!

2 CORINITHIANS 10:4-5

For the weapons of our warfare are not of the flesh, but divinely powerful for the destruction of fortresses. 5 We are destroying speculations and every lofty thing raised up against the knowledge of God, and we are taking every thought captive to the obedience of Christ.

THE BIBLE IS MY MIRROR!

2 CORINITHIANS 3:18

But we all, with unveiled face beholding as in a mirror the glory of the Lord, are being transformed into the same image from glory to glory, just as from the Lord, the spirit.

GOD IS PLEASED WITH ME!

PSALM 147:11

The Lord is pleased with those who worship Him and trust His love.

Slow down and relax, Shelly.

SLOW DOWN AND RELAX SHELLY. HURRYING AFFECTS MY SPIRITUAL LIFE

JESUS CAME SO THAT I MAY HAVE PEACE!

JOHN 16:33 Jesus said:

"These things I have spoken to you, that in Me you may have peace. In the world you have tribulation, but take courage; I have overcome the world".

Peace I leave with you; My peace I now give and bequeth to you. Not as the world gives do I give to you. Do not let your hearts be troubled, neither let them be afraid. JOHN14:27

It is God's desire that I be free of all anxiety and distressing care. 7:32

Do not be anxious about anything. Instead in every situation through prayer and petition with thanksgiving tell my request to God and the peace of God that surpasses all understanding will guard your hearts and minds in Jesus Christ. Philippians 4:6-7

Live like Jesus did! Stop allowing myself to be agitated and disturbed and do not permit myself to be fearful and intimidated and cowardly and unsettled.

GOD WILL MEET ALL MY NEEDS

PHILIPIANS 4:19

19And my God will meet all your needs according to his glorious riches in Christ Jesus.

Declare that my needs are met because the word says so!

2 CORINITHIANS 6:3

MATTHEW 6:6

6But when you pray, go into your room, close the door and pray to your Father, who is unseen. Then your Father, who sees what is done in secret, will reward you.

7Submit yourselves, then, to God. Resist the devil, and he will flee from you.

7Submit yourselves, then, to God. Resist the devil, and he will flee from you.

PHILIPIANS 1:6

6being confident of this, that he who began a good work in you will carry it on to completion until the day of Christ Jesus.

I don't have to work at God's plan for me, he will cause it to come to pass

BE CAREFUL HOW I LIVE

EPHESIANS 5:15

Living by the Spirit's Power

15 So be careful how you live. Don't live like fools, but like those who are wise. 16 Make the most of every opportunity in these evil days. 17 Don't act thoughtlessly, but understand what the Lord wants you to do. 18 Don't be drunk with wine, because that will ruin your life. Instead, be filled with the Holy Spirit, 19 singing psalms and hymns and spiritual songs among yourselves, and making music to the Lord in your hearts. 20 And give thanks for everything to God the Father in the name of our Lord Jesus Christ.

I AM GODS SERVANT

2 CORINITHIANS 6

Rather as servants of God we commend ourselves in every way in great endurance (in troubles, hardships and distress)

I AM FREE FOREVER FROM CONDEMNATION

ROMANS 8:1-2

Therefore, there is now no condemnation for those who are in Christ Jesus, 2because through Christ Jesus the law of the Spirit of life set me free from the law of sin and death.

Appendix E: My Purpose

There are many Bible verses that have helped sustain me. For those of you who are facing difficulties, here are some of my recommendations:

PRAYERS FOR BEGINNING THE DAY

Suggested prayer: "Dear God, please help me to discover my God-given life purpose, get well-trained for it, and with your help dedicate my life to fulfilling it. Thank you for hearing and answering my prayer.

Just for Today

Today remember who is in charge and planning only for you. A day filled with love, direction, connection, and spiritual and emotional healing. There is a plan and it is much better than anything I could orchestrate. Remember to listen to that still small voice inside and be willing and open to take direction throughout today while clinging to gratefulness, and focusing on strengthening that.

Just for today, live in today and remain engrossed in your present moment while being careful and mindful of your thoughts.

Whatever you do today, give it all of your love and attention, and gratefully accept whatever and whoever God puts in your path.

PSALM 32:8 NI

I will instruct you and teach you in the way you should go; I will counsel you with my loving eye on you.

Ask God to direct my thinking, especially that it be divorced from self-pity, dishonest, or self-seeking motives. When I am unsure and not able to determine which course to take, I ask God for inspiration, intuitive thought, or decision. Relax, Shelly. Right answers will come.

PAGE 77 AA Big Book

Our real purpose is to fit ourselves to be of maximum service to God and the people about us.

MAKE LOVING GOD & SERVING GOD MY #1 PURPOSE AND HE WILL TAKE CARE OF EVERYTHING ELSE. ROMANS 8:12

And we know that in all things God works for the good of those who love him who have been called according to his purpose.

I WAS CREATED TO SERVE

EPHESIANS 2: 10 (NLT)

For we are God's workmanship, created in Christ Jesus to do good works, which God prepared in advance for us to do.

I AM GOD'S SERVANT

2 CORINITHIANS 6:4

Rather, as servants of God we commend ourselves in every way: in great endurance; in troubles, hardships and distresses;

ROMANS 6:16 (KJV)

16 Know ye not, that to whom ye yield yourselves servants to obey, his servants ye are to whom ye obey; whether of sin unto death, or of obedience unto righteousness?

We can obey God or obey Satan.

MATTHEW 20:26-28

27 And whoever wants to be first among you must be your slave. 28 Just as the Son of Man did not did not come to be served but to serve, and to give His life as a ransom for many.

CREATE TO LOVE

MATTHEW 22:36-39

36 Teacher, which is the greatest commandment in the Law?" 37 Jesus replied: "Love the Lord your God with all your heart and with all your soul and with all your mind. 38 This is the first and greatest commandment. 39 And the second is like it: Love your neighbor as yourself. 40 All the Law and the Prophets hang on these two commandments."

ROMANS 12:10, 11

Be devoted to one another in brotherly love; give preference to one another in honor; not lagging behind in diligence, fervent in serving the Lord;

MAKE SERVING GOD MY #1 PURPOSE AND HE WILL TAKE CARE OF EVERYTHING ELSE!

ROMANS 11:36

For everything comes from God alone. Everything lives by His power and everything is for His glory.

SERVICE IS NOT OPTIONAL!

ROMANS 9:17

For the Scripture says to Pharaoh: "I raised you up for this very purpose, that I might display my power in you and that my name might be proclaimed in all the earth."[a]

1 CORITHIANS 9:19-23

TO SERVE I MUST ADAPT AND ADJUST TO MINISTER TO OTHERS! BE SENSITIVE TO PEOPLES NEEDS

19 Though I am free and belong to no man, I make myself a slave to everyone, to win as many as possible. 20 To the Jews I became like a Jew, to win the Jews. To those under the law I became like one under the law (though I myself am not under the law), so as to win those under the law. 21 To those not having the law I became like one not having the law (though I am not free from God's law but am under Christ's law), so as to win those not having the law. 22 To the weak I became weak, to win the weak. I have become all things to all men so that by all possible means I might save some. 23 I do all this for the sake of the gospel, that I may share in its blessings

1 TIMOTHY 4:12

BE AN EXAMPLE

2 CORINITHIANS 9:12 NIV

THE SERVICE I PERFORM....

12 This service that you perform is not only supplying the needs of God's people but is also overflowing in many expressions of thanks to God.

CREATED TO LOVE

JOHN 13:34

A new command I give you: Love one another. As I have loved you, so you must love one another.

JOHN 15:9

As the Father has loved me, so have I loved you. Now remain in my love.

JOHN 15:12

My command is this: Love each other as I have loved you.

Monday, March 19, 2018 DON'T FORGET IT, SHELLY!!

I WAS CREATED FOR WORSHIP AND TO GIVE THANKS

ECCLESIATES 12:13

After all this, there is only one thing to say, have reverence for God and obey His commands because this is all we were created for, worship.

1 THESSALONIANS 5:16-18

REJOICE ALWAYS

16 Rejoice always, 17 pray continually, 18 give thanks in all circumstances; for this is God's will for you in Christ Jesus.

GIVE THANKS IN WORSHIP

PSALM 100:4

Enter his gates with thanksgiving and his courts with praise; give thanks to him and praise his name

PHILIPPIANS 4:4-7

IN PRAYER

Think of Excellence

4 Rejoice in the Lord always; again I will say, rejoice! 5 let your gentle spirit be known to all men. The Lord is near. 6 Be anxious for nothing, but in everything by prayer and supplication with thanksgiving let your requests be made known to God. 7 And the peace of God, which surpasses all comprehension, will guard your hearts and your minds in Christ Jesus. 8 Finally, brethren, whatever is true, whatever is honorable, whatever is right, whatever is pure, whatever is lovely, whatever is of good repute, if there is any excellence and if anything worthy of praise, dwell on these things. 9 The things you have learned and received and heard and seen in me, practice these things, and the God of peace will be with you.

IN EVERYTHING

1 THESSALONIANS 5:18 NIV

18 give thanks in all circumstances, for this is God's will for you in Christ Jesus.

IN EVERYTHING AGAIN

EPHESIANS 5:20

20 always giving thanks to God the Father for everything, in the name of our Lord Jesus Christ.

IN DAILY LIVING

COLOSSIANS 2:6-7

Spiritual Fullness in Christ. So then, just as you received Christ Jesus as Lord, continue to live your lives in him, 7 rooted and built up in him, strengthened in the faith as you were taught, and overflowing with thankfulness. So then, just as you received Christ Jesus as Lord, continue to live in him, 7 rooted and built up in him, strengthened in the faith as you were taught, and overflowing with thankfulness.

IN GIVING

2 CORINITHIANS 9:12 NIV

12 This service that you perform is not only supplying the needs of God's people but is also overflowing in many expressions of thanks to God.

IN SPIRITUAL BATTLES

1 CORINTHIANS 15:55-57NIV

55 "Where, O death, is your victory? Where, O death, is your sting? 56 The sting of death is sin, and the power of sin is the law. 57 But thanks be to God! He gives us the victory through our Lord Jesus Christ.

IN FRIENDSHIPS

PHILIPPIANS 1:1-3

1 Paul and Timothy, servants of Christ Jesus, To all the saints in Christ Jesus at Philippi, together with the overseers[a] and deacons: 2 Grace and peace to you from God our Father and the Lord Jesus Christ. Thanksgiving and Prayer 3 I thank my God every time I remember you.

1 CORINITHIANS 3:18

I WAS CREATED TO BECOME LIKE CHRIST!

As the spirit of the Lord works within us, we become more and more like Him and reflect His glory even more.

2 CORITHIANS 10:4-5

ALIGN MY THINKING WITH GOD'S

4 The weapons we fight with are not the weapons of the world. On the contrary, they have divine power to demolish strongholds. 5 We demolish arguments and every pretension that sets itself up against the knowledge of God, and we take captive every thought to make it obedient to Christ.

1 CORITHIANS 16:9 "NEW LEVEL OF SPIRITUALITY, NEW DEVIL"

For a wide door for effective service has been opened to me, and there are many adversaries

EPHESIANS 5:15

LIVE LIFE WITH A DUE SENSE OF RESPONSIBILITY, NOT AS THOSE WHO DO NOT KNOW THE MEANING OF LIFE BUT THOSE WHO DO.

15 Be very careful, then, how you live—not as unwise but as wise, 16 making the most of every opportunity, because the days are evil. 17 Therefore do not be foolish, but understand what the Lord's will is. 18 Do

not get drunk on wine, which leads to debauchery. Instead, be filled with the Spirit. 19 Speak to one another with psalms, hymns and spiritual songs. Sing and make music in your heart to the Lord, 20 always giving thanks to God the Father for everything, in the name of our Lord Jesus Christ. 21 Submit to one another out of reverence for Christ.

1 CORINITHIANS 12:6

6 There are different kinds of working, but the same God works all of them in all men.

1 PETER 3:8-98

SUFFERING FOR DOING GOOD

Finally, all of you, live in harmony with one another; be sympathetic, love as brothers, be compassionate and humble. 9 Do not repay evil with evil or insult with insult, but with blessing, because to this you were called so that you may inherit a blessing.

PHILIPIANS 2:1-11

IMITATE CHRIST'S HUMILITY, SERVE OTHERS

1 If you have any encouragement from being united with Christ, if any comfort from his love, if any fellowship with the Spirit, if any tenderness and compassion, 2 then make my joy complete by being like-minded, having the same love, being one in spirit and purpose. 3 Do nothing out of selfish ambition or vain conceit, but in humility consider others better than yourselves. 4 Each of you should look not only to your own interests, but also to the interests of others.

5 Your attitude should be the same as that of Christ Jesus: 6 Who, being in very nature[a] God, did not consider equality with God something to be grasped, 7 but made himself nothing, taking the very nature[b] of a servant, being made in human likeness. 8 And being found in appearance as a man, he humbled himself and became obedient to death— even death on a cross! 9 Therefore God exalted him to the highest place and gave him the name that is above every name, 10 that at the name of Jesus every

knee should bow, in heaven and on earth and under the earth, 11 and every tongue confess that Jesus Christ is Lord, to the glory of God the Father.

GIVE THANKS AND PRAISE

PHILIPPIANS 4:4-9

4 Rejoice in the Lord always. I will say it again: Rejoice! 5 Let your gentleness be evident to all. The Lord is near. 6 Do not be anxious about anything, but in everything, by prayer and petition, with thanksgiving, present your requests to God. 7 And the peace of God, which transcends all understanding, will guard your hearts and your minds in Christ Jesus.

8 Finally, brothers, whatever is true, whatever is noble, whatever is right, whatever is pure, whatever is lovely, whatever is admirable—if anything is excellent or praiseworthy—think about such things. 9 Whatever you have learned or received or heard from me, or seen in me—put it into practice. And the God of peace will be with you.

HEBREWS 13:15

15 Through Jesus, therefore, let us _continually_ offer to God a sacrifice of praise—the fruit of lips that confess his name. (GIVE THANKS CONSTANTLY and in all things.)

COLOSSIONS 3 1-17 (NIV)

Rules for Holy Living

1 Since, then, you have been raised with Christ, set your hearts on things above, where Christ is seated at the right hand of God. 2 Set your minds on things above, not on earthly things. 3 For you died, and your life is now hidden with Christ in God. 4 When Christ, who is your[a] life, appears, then you also will appear with him in glory.

5 Put to death, therefore, whatever belongs to your earthly nature: sexual immorality, impurity, lust, evil desires and greed, which is idolatry. 6 Because of these, the wrath of God is coming.[b] 7 You used to walk in

these ways, in the life you once lived. 8 But now you must rid yourselves of all such things as these: anger, rage, malice, slander, and filthy language from your lips. 9 Do not lie to each other, since you have taken off your old self with its practices 10 and have put on the new self, which is being renewed in knowledge in the image of its Creator. 11 Here there is no Greek or Jew, circumcised or uncircumcised, barbarian, Scythian, slave or free, but Christ is all, and is in all.

12 Therefore, as God's chosen people, holy and dearly loved, clothe yourselves with compassion, kindness, humility, gentleness and patience. 13 Bear with each other and forgive whatever grievances you may have against one another. Forgive as the Lord forgave you. 14 And over all these virtues put on love, which binds them all together in perfect unity.

15 Let the peace of Christ rule in your hearts, since as members of one body you were called to peace. And be thankful. 16 Let the word of Christ dwell in you richly as you teach and admonish one another with all wisdom, and as you sing psalms, hymns and spiritual songs with gratitude in your hearts to God. 17 And whatever you do, whether in word or deed, do it all in the name of the Lord Jesus, giving thanks to God the Father through him.

HEBREWS 10:25

Not forsaking the assembling of ourselves together as is the manner of some, but exhorting one another, and so much the more as you see the Day approaching.

Exhort -: to incite by argument or advice: urge strongly <exhorting voters to do the right thing>intransitive verb: to give warnings or advice: make urgent appeals

Made in the USA
Middletown, DE
27 February 2023